T0083462

ENRAGED CITIZENS, EUROPEAN PEACE AND DEMOCRATIC DEFICITS

THE GERMAN LIST

RECENT TITLES FROM THE GERMAN LIST

THOMAS BERNHARD
Goethe Dies

KLAUS HOFFER
Among the Bieresch

CHRISTOPH RANSMAYR
Atlas of an Anxious Man

WERNER BRÄUNIG
Rummelplatz

HANS MAGNUS ENZENSBERGER
Mr Zed's Reflections

ANSELM KEIFER
Notebooks, Volume 1: 1998–99

ALEXANDER KLUGE
*30 April 1945: The Day Hitler Shot Himself and Germany's Integration
with the West Began*

WOLFGANG HILBIG
'I'

GEORG TRAKL
Poems
Sebastian Dreaming

ROBERT MENASSE

**ENRAGED CITIZENS, EUROPEAN PEACE
AND DEMOCRATIC DEFICITS**

Or Why the Democracy Given to Us
Must Become One We Fight For

TRANSLATED BY CRAIG DECKER

LONDON NEW YORK CALCUTTA

This publication was supported by grants from the the Goethe-Institut India and the Austrian Federal Ministry for Education, the Arts and Culture.

Seagull Books, 2016

Originally published in German as *Der Europäische Landbote: Die Wut der Bürger und der Friede Europas oder Warum die geschenkte Demokratie einer erkämpften weichen muss*

© Paul Zsolnay Verlag, Vienna, 2012

First published in English translation by Seagull Books, 2016.

English translation © Craig Decker, 2016

ISBN 978 0 85742 362 7

British Library Cataloguing-in-Publication Data
A catalogue record for this book is available from the British Library.

Typeset in Scala and ScalaSans by Seagull Books, Calcutta, India
Printed and bound by Maple Press, York, Pennsylvania, USA

*Thinking about the
Occident at night.*

CONTENTS

1

Enraged Citizens, European Peace and Democratic Deficits

112

Postscript

131

Glossary

1

If you take a black marker to the map of Europe and plot all the political borders that have ever existed there over the course of recorded history, then by the time you are finished you will end up with such a dense network covering the continent that it will be an almost completely black surface. Which black line within that black surface can be obviously considered a natural border?

If you then take a red marker and draw lines on the map connecting the belligerent parties and marking the battlefields and progression of the fronts in every war that ever occurred in Europe, then that network of borders will completely disappear beneath the red area.

2

Since I've begun to write this essay, a Facebook friend from Hannover, Germany, a well-read and politically engaged man, has posted: 'The EU will be our demise!' Countless 'friends' have immediately responded with 'likes'.

Yes! The EU will be our demise! And that's a good thing, too!

With this essay, I would like to try to explain why.

Before starting to criticize the European Union—and there's certainly plenty well worth debating and criticizing—

it's important to keep in mind the map of Europe outlined above, that blood-soaked surface beneath which empires, nations and cities have repeatedly disappeared. And one should also remember the historical rationale for launching the project that ultimately became today's EU.

It's common knowledge that in the middle of the last century, Europe was once again lying in ruins. Four wars in the course of a single lifetime—the Austro-Prussian War (1866) and the Franco-Prussian War (1870–71), both of which were so-called wars of national unification, and then, especially, the two European wars that became world wars and that, for all intents and purposes, amounted to a 'second Thirty Years War' (1914–45)—had devastated the continent to an unprecedented extent. The ideology of the autonomous, self-assertive and autocratic nation; the dynamics of nationalism; the 'age-old animosity' among nations; and the attempt to assert by hook or by crook one's 'national interests' over those of other nations has claimed the lives of countless millions, caused endless human suffering, and, culminating in the unbridled nationalism signified by the word 'Auschwitz', led to atrocious crimes against humanity.

There was virtually nothing left. The infrastructure was largely destroyed, industries severely damaged or confiscated, and resources and goods were scarce. Money was tight. The situation was such that even the grandparents of today's intransigents could clearly recognize: this must never be allowed to happen again. If it's possible to overcome the misery, then it must be done in such a way that the catastrophes caused by nationalism and conflicting national interests will never be repeated.

Peace treaties between nations—so experience taught—were not worth the paper they were printed on. The nations, according to the vision of the founding fathers of the European peace project, must become institutionally and economically so intertwined, so mutually dependent that the pursuit of any self-interest could only be possible through joint action. Only in this way could solidarity (as opposed to nationalistic hatred), permanent peace and collective prosperity be attained.

The historical rationale for the subsequent EU also lies in the bloodstained aspiration to transcend nationalism through a postnational development organized and impelled by supranational institutions. The OEEC, the Organisation for European Economic Co-operation,* created the first supranational institution in Europe in 1947, under the control of the USA. It dispensed the funds of the Marshall Plan and coordinated the economic and financial programmes of the states participating in it. Nowadays it is frequently forgotten that, at the time, it wasn't merely the fact that there was support and aid for the physically devastated and economically bankrupt nations. It was the synchronized, supranational economic policy that fundamentally enabled the reconstruction and economic recovery of the European countries. Shortly after the founding of the OEEC, the initial independent European supranational institution was created: the Montanunion,* or

---

* See Glossary for all terms marked with asterisks.

European Coal and Steel Community (ECSC), in 1951. It was established by six European countries (Germany, France, Belgium, Italy, Luxembourg and the Netherlands), which, just a few years earlier, had considered one another enemies and treated one another as aggressors or victims. Now, they jointly established a 'High Authority', which, in the realm of the coal and steel industries, set common policies for all member states. Why, of all things, coal and steel? They were essential raw materials for both the war and postwar reconstruction. To communalize their production and distribution and bring it under shared control was thus equally desirable for keeping the peace and for the economic recovery of war-torn Europe.

With that, Europe's postnational development was definitively launched, leading to greater and bolder steps as well as many smaller ones—from the Treaties of Rome,* the Maastricht Treaty* and the Treaty of Lisbon* to today's European Union.

In my experience, most people get bored whenever the history of the EU is recounted, even in its most abbreviated form. I, on the other hand, am fond of that particular boredom, and I don't wish for myself or for anyone else the extremely exciting history that would no doubt result from the break-up of the EU and a relapse into a Europe of competing nations.

Whoever considers the current crisis of the EU, the so-called financial crisis induced by Greece's budget deficits, as unsolvable through solidarity, and whoever considers the current necessary and systematic steps towards European unification as unfeasible on account of public opinion should think back to the beginning of the development and try to imagine the following: in order to establish the supranational High Authority of the European Coal and Steel Community, it was necessary for France to relinquish sovereignty rights to Germany. What must the sentiments in France have been like? France had just been occupied and humiliated by Germany, but was now liberated and a victorious power; Germany, in the public opinion of the French, was a gang of criminals at long last subjugated.

It was bold. It was risky. It was, right up to the end, extremely close. It was, however, possible to create a majority in the French parliament against public opinion, one in favour of interlocking France's economic interests with those of Germany and also subjecting French economic policy to a controlling body that included Germany. That state of affairs should now be remembered with the utmost gratitude, especially in Germany.

Back then people of great political stature were involved. For them, the slogan 'No more war, no more Auschwitz' was not a boring cliché or an annoying mantra. Due to their experiences and traumas, it was the literal and essential inspiration for their political efforts.

Let us take another step back, all the way to the beginning. What was the sentiment like in West Germany when the OEEC was founded? Obviously, the Federal Republic of Germany desperately needed the capital that was coming from the USA. But public opinion was far from enthusiastic and gratefully affirmative. The Germans had lost the war and were disillusioned by their rants about the master race. But to now have to accept gifts from the victors—gifts that were not exactly selfless—induced a collective sense of humiliation among large segments of the German population, leading to truculence. Last but not least, it also induced the fear, occasioned by their military defeat, of having to lose not only their political sovereignty but also their national cultural identity. Prominent German philosophers, ones truly beyond suspicion of being National Socialist sympathizers, concurred with 'public sentiments' when they groused about jazz, that American 'Negro music'. Upstanding German fathers forbade their children to drink Coca-Cola, disseminating—as they guzzled steins of beer with their drinking buddies—modern legends about the corrosive effects of that American drink on one's liver. Leading German pedagogues mounted an enormous campaign—which seeped through the media and parent–teacher organizations into the living rooms of German nuclear families—against the schlock that was Mickey Mouse comic books. The flowing capital was met with vehement and cantankerous cultural clashes.

Following their experience with the only recently dampened Nazi fervour of the Germans, Konrad Adenauer and the political elites of the time realized with profound disillusionment that vox populi is by no means synonymous with vox Dei. They also learnt, quicker than their constituents, that the institutionalized practices of democracy carry political responsibilities that need to be understood independent of popular economic sentiments. If, at that point in time in West Germany, opinion polls had played a decisive role in governmental decisions, then West Germany would have become an agrarian state, conceivably the leading potato exporter in the world.

3

From its beginnings, the EU was, of course, an elitist project. The founders of Europe's supranational institutions understood that lasting peace on the continent could only be achieved by transcending nationalism. That meant that nationalism must not just be 'tamed' somehow, domesticated to flag-waving festivities at international sporting events. The soil nourishing nationalism must be completely eradicated. And that soil was the nation-state. The utopia was that the nation-states, through the intertwining of their economies, would be compelled to relinquish their sovereignty step by step, increasingly rolling back the nation-states until they ultimately withered away, absorbed into a borderless Europe. Only in that way would it be possible to create a peace that the nation-states couldn't conceive of as an interwar period during which they would arm themselves for the next war so that they could then once again militarily assert their political and economic interests.

Even back then the notion of the eventual withering away of the nation-states was not supported by the majority, though the cataclysmic lessons they learnt from nationalism were still quite fresh in their minds and the consequences of nationalistic frenzy were clearly apparent to all. No matter how sensible the idea is, nowadays it appears even less acceptable to the majority. And so we arrive at the heart of the problem we now refer to as 'the European crisis'. Many details of the crisis are familiar to everyone, but its substance remains misunderstood.

An elitist project. That, of course, sounds horrible to democratic ears. But does the term really express a democratic, politically grounded mistrust? As a matter of fact, the denunciation of the EU as an 'elitist project' does not give expression to many people's fear of losing their ability to participate in the political process—decreasing voter turnouts, even in national elections, speak volumes. It instead expresses a defensive attitude towards losing their national identity. 'Elitist' does not—and never did—stand in opposition to 'democracy' (at least—and that's so obvious it doesn't need any supporting evidence—in the bourgeois democracies of the nation-states) but, rather, to the 'masses', and that particular opposition has traditionally been subsumed by the 'people' in 'national identity'.

Criticizing the democratic deficit of the EU gives expression to an anxiety about the insidious loss of an identity that, objectively, has always been a chimera, but one capable of holding the elites and the people together—while also delimiting them from the others—within a nation. That explains why all the following things are currently happening: increased criticism of Europe's democratic deficit, rage directed at one's 'own' elites who are internationally involved and active, and increased renationalization.

4

If you had the choice between (a) a sovereign nation-state that represented your national interests through orderly, constitutional processes and (b) a bureaucratic juggernaut, founded and led by elites who, in their inscrutable mania for regulation, wanted to homogenize the various European cultures and then forced you to support with your taxes a corrupt, alien state full of tax frauds—which one would you choose?

You would . . . Forget about it, we know the answer! But what you don't take into account is how much of that seemingly innocent 'democratic' decision depends on the formulation of the choice and your ability to question it. What, for instance, are 'national interests'? Can you please explain to me what your justifiable 'national interests' are, and in such a way that it's immediately comprehensible to me that only you as, let's say, a member of the German nation have good reason to have those interests while not a single Portuguese, no one from Holland, no Italian and no Lithuanian can have those interests? Can you please name for me those of your interests that are legitimate in terms of human rights and, at the same time, singular in Europe and the rest of the world? What could they be? Isn't it more likely that everything you could identify as your plausible interest would be just as plausible to the Portuguese, the Greeks, the Dutch, etc.?

Is it a problem for you that the EU is an elitist project and not the expression of the 'people's will'? What about the following formulation: If you could choose between (a) a nation-state financed through your tax monies that essentially represents the interests of a small group of national political and economic elites who are even prepared to assert those interests using force if necessary and (b) a free association of free citizens whose supranational institutions protect their civil rights and liberties and secure the peace no matter where they live on the continent, no matter where they travel to and no matter where they settle down to earn their living?

As I said, they're just formulations.

But the one to which the large majority spontaneously nods is more ridiculous than the somewhat glossed-over other one.

5

Typically, the ridiculous thing about the formulations used to express a sceptical or even hostile attitude towards the EU is that they characterize issues on a European level as 'menacing' or 'scandalous' which on a national level are perceived, or at least accepted, as being completely 'natural' and 'rational'. What's simply called 'legislation' on a national level is pejoratively referred to as a 'mania for regulation' in the European unification process. That federal laws apply to all states and regions within a nation is self-evident, whereas European guidelines and ordinances are described as 'homogenizing diverse cultures and mentalities' and rejected as 'crazy', 'senseless' and 'authoritarian' by an increasing number of people. I'm not familiar with any critique of German federal legislation that argues that it levels and homogenizes the diverse cultures and mentalities of Prussia, Bavaria, Hesse, Franconia, Saxony, etc. Conversely, it's completely incomprehensible why sensible social parameters that work for Bavarians and Hessians couldn't also work for Slovenes, Carinthians, Catalonians, South Tyroleans, etc. The German experience has allegedly demonstrated that a diversity of cultures and mentalities by no means disappears if they are given common parameters for their respective developments. We are talking about parameters here. As we know from experience, within those parameters states and regions can develop according to their respective specifics. The autonomy of regional cultures and mentalities can only ever really be threatened, repressed or falsified if national identity is subsumed by the notion of a national *Volkskörper*.

Here's another example: Why, of all places, in the FRG* (subsequently unified with the GDR*), which has become the nation of GZSZ,* DSDS* and GNTM,* the country in which the commonly used four-letter word 'Auto' had to be reduced to a three-letter abbreviation, 'Kfz',* which must be inspected by the TÜV* and whose drivers are members of ADAC*—why must people there insist with such supercilious scorn that the European Union suffers from an 'abbreviation mania'? It constantly produces acronyms, they claim, which its citizens simply can't understand. Such an excess of abbreviations that you shouldn't be surprised its citizens turn away, uncomprehendingly and disinterested. It's odd. It didn't require the EU for a series of abbreviations to establish themselves as comprehensible and natural in everyday speech, provided you have frequent contact with them. And if that's not the case, then it's never really been a problem for you. The Austrian Federal Ministry of Education, the Arts and Culture, for example, is known as the 'BMUKK' in German, lovingly and ironically called 'Bumukl' by Austrian artists. It could well be that a steelworker in Linz can't make any sense of that particular abbreviation, but that steelworker certainly knows what ÖGB (the Austrian Trade Union Federation) means.

Why is that which in every other state is simply called the 'administration' is almost always called a 'dictatorship of civil servants' or a 'bureaucratic juggernaut' in discussions about the EU? Every old cliché about civil servants and every stereotypical prejudice about public officials are now projected onto 'Brussels'. The European bureaucracy is to blame for any and all grievances, deficits, problems, contradictions and frustrations. Everything is always a mania: a 'mania for regulations', an 'abbreviation mania'. . . . 'The EU' at present appears in the public's perception as a monstrous, bloated bureaucracy; the civil servant, entrenched in the fortress, as the fundamental evil. Any reflection on the contemporary condition of Europe must therefore begin with an examination of its bureaucrats.

6

Perhaps it was a quirky idea, but pursuing it for a while was extremely instructive. The idea was to write a novel set in Brussels, whose main character was an official with the European Commission.* If it's still possible to write a realist novel that, through its manifestations of reality, depicts the essence of an epoch, then (such was my thought process) I had best make my way to the place where that reality is being produced—and, without a doubt, that place nowadays is Brussels. There, in the reviled 'bureaucratic palaces', our actual and essential social parameters are being established, no matter where on the continent we are located. Who are those bureaucrats, those new types of civil servants, for whom—and in order to differentiate them from conventional state officials—a distinct term was coined: the 'Eurocrats'? Do they have a face? Can you categorize them? What does their daily routine look like? And how do they reach their decisions? I didn't yet have a plot. But to get things started, I did need to know: Is the engine room producing our reality suitable for a novel? And are the people working in it 'characters'? So I flew to Brussels, rented a flat and, in the subsequent weeks and months, tried to meet as many Eurocrats as possible—talk with them, have them tell me about their work and life, and, if possible (and it was possible), observe them working.

7

Among all the monsters—from the basilisk to Count Dracula to King Kong—the public official assumes a particularly prominent place. Its fantasized being is not merely the product of the anxiously lusting dreams of the individual philistine who must repeatedly fantasize his or her own danger and demise so as to ultimately be able to dream about a felicitous salvation. The fantasized public official is truly a phenomenon of society as a whole. The character of the civil servant is constituted from the negative images of all social classes, trade groups and professions: the civil servant is privileged while as unsophisticated as a provincial aristocrat; displays lower-middle-class stolidity and pigheadedness; is as addicted to regulations as a labour representative and, at the same time, as indolent as a member of the lumpenproletariat. As bigoted and perfidiously clever as a peasant, the civil servant can concoct nonsense as creatively as any entrepreneur who cunningly creates the demands he or she then claims to be able to meet; and, like all welfare cheats, is obsessed with reproducing him- or herself savagely and at the taxpayers' expense.

It's amazing how this artificial figure, this pieced-together fiction, wanders like a ghost with sustained success through the collective imagination, never collapsing to death in the light of day. In contrast to Count Dracula, for instance, everyone has met a public official in reality. Furthermore, if you divide the average family size by the proportional amount of civil servants within the adult population, then statistically two out of every three people must have a father, an uncle, an aunt, a sister, a father-in-law, or, at the very least, one other close relative who works in the civil service. There is no other profession with which more than two-thirds of the European population has such close family ties. (Germany and Austria lie in the statistical middle.) One of the greatest sociological enigmas is why that empirical fact and the concrete experiences resulting from it do not lead to eliminating the unrealistic mental image of the civil servant wandering through the collective imagination—or at least, better aligning that image with reality.

Having said that, one substantial change has recently occurred regarding the image of the civil servant. When most people now think of a 'civil servant', they no longer think about a magistrate in their hometown or a ministry official in their state capital, nor do they think about their child's teacher or a police officer they've met on the street. Instead, they immediately think of the 'bureaucracy in Brussels'. Eurobarometer surveys clearly indicate how closely many citizens associate the EU with 'bureaucracy'—and vice versa. 'In the consciousness of Europe's citizens, the EU is a remote, bureaucratic juggernaut.' The main reason for their 'Euroscepticism' (36 per cent of those surveyed in 2011) or 'rejection of the EU' (42 per cent) was that 'far-reaching political decisions were made by officials lacking political legitimacy'. More than 70 per cent of those surveyed had a 'very negative' or 'somewhat negative' attitude towards European officials. As to the rationale (multiple answers were possible), the majority cited: 'overregulation and beureau-cratization', 'aloofness' and 'privileges'. Nowadays, 'Brussels bureaucracy' is the catch-all that many people repeatedly and generally use to express that which, in their day-to-day experiences or in their consumption of the media, provokes criticism, resentment or rage.

Nowadays, it's clear that reality has even less of a chance of correcting the fantasy image of the civil servant given that the remote Brussels Eurocrat has superseded the home-grown official as the epitome of the public servant. At the same time, the emergence of the Brussels bureaucracy has not only 'transported', as it were, the civil servant, it has also fundamentally redefined him or her—but that transformation has yet to enter the public consciousness. The Brussels bureaucrat is not only socially perceived as an Other, he or she is simultaneously—and primarily—an Other in the classical sense of the term. The person no longer serves a public institution belonging to his or her nation and no longer swears loyalty to the nation but, instead, serves a supranational institution, such as the European Commission, whose task is to push back the special interests of the individual nations and ultimately overcome the nation-states, including the one the official comes from. The Brussels bureaucrat, along with the bureaucratic apparatus of the European Commission, works for the common interests and towards communalizing the parameters of the current 28 member states, and thus consistently against the government of his or her own country as well as against all national bureaucracies. We're therefore dealing with a bureaucracy that contradicts traditional bureaucracies. Historically, the Brussels bureaucracy constitutes a completely new type. It is the first one not bound to its ruler or its government, and the first one to consistently call state bureaucracies into question and, when appropriate, correct or rescind their policies and decisions. That alone is a fascinating state of affairs. Moreover, it's an expression of great historical reasoning if you consider the devastation resulting from the blind 'administration' of so-called national interests, to which the European unification process represents the historical answer. But even I learnt that only after having moved to Brussels to get to know the 'bureaucrats'—the real ones, that is, in the flesh and in person.

8

I encountered one surprise after another, as if there had been a secret agreement to debunk all the clichés and fantasies about the Eurocrats and invert them in reality.

My first surprise: the Commission is an open and transparent institution. I discovered open doors and bureaucrats eager to impart information. And if, in the corridors of the Berlaymont building,* you suddenly encounter a series of closed doors, then that's an exception and you're in the Directorate General for Culture. But that's another story.

My second surprise: the Brussels bureaucracy is extremely lean. To administer the entire continent, the EU has fewer officials at its disposal than the number working for the city of Vienna alone.

My third surprise: the Brussels bureaucracy is extremely frugal and modest. The officials' offices, even on the upper floors of the hierarchy, are functional and nothing else. There are no luxuries and hardly any amenities.

My fourth surprise: the Brussels bureaucracy is incredibly cheap. The European Union has a budget that amounts to 1 per cent of the European gross national product (GNP). To administer an entire continent and fulfil all their responsibilities, the institutions of the EU (the 'bureaucracy', that is) have access to 6 per cent of that budget annually; that amounts to merely 0.06 per cent of the European GNP. There is not another state administrative apparatus or another sizeable political project that is so cheap. The costs of German unification, for instance, amounted (and still amount) to 4 per cent of the West German GNP per annum. (That, by the way, provides an interesting example of how great the difference is between the price of national and European consciousness. For German national consciousness, the costs of German unification are not too high, and if they are, then necessarily so. The costs for

European consciousness, on the other hand, appear astronomic. For European consciousness, the costs of European communitarization are astoundingly modest; the costs for the unification of the two German states, however, are largely a substantial waste of money. If the GDR had joined the EU, avoiding the detour of a greater German national rebirth, the modernization of the GDR using EU subsidies would have been considerably cheaper and would have proceeded far less humiliatingly.)

My fifth surprise: the bureaucrats are funny. I hardly ever met any humourless or rigid, old fossils. Through their work on the European project, the characteristics of their respective national identities have turned into quirks they treat self-deprecatingly. Or, to put it another way: freed from national beastliness, a mentality can turn into a culture.

Occasionally, I saw in those people who concretely disproved the fictional image of the bureaucrat but were themselves another kind of fiction, a new one. In their practice, their work and how they structure their lives, they're frequently what would no doubt be attractive to become, that is, truly European: polyglot, highly qualified, enlightened and rooted in the cultures they come from yet liberated from the irrationality of a so-called national identity.

Maybe that's not a fiction at all but, rather, the 2.0 version of the Josephinian bureaucracy* which in its multinational reach can, on a certain level, be considered a precursor to the present European administration. With all due criticism of the Habsburg monarchy and with all due mistrust of its subsequent idealization, the merits of Josephinism and the Habsburg bureaucracy are still evident, even in the former Crown lands— almost a century after the demise of that multi-ethnic state.

That's right, the educated EU critics will now respond. Wasn't the proposition 'Everything for the people, nothing by the people' the motto of the Josephinian administration? And doesn't that point to exactly the same problem? That bureaucrats lacking political legitimacy want to decide what's best for the general public? It doesn't matter how well intentioned the guidelines concocted by the Commission's bureaucrats are— no one elected them; they are simply not legitimate.

We are talking about civil servants. Civil servants are not elected. Not even in Germany. There are various possibilities for guaranteeing the democratic legitimacy of a system. Of course, the democratic legitimacy of the EU can be established primarily through strengthening the European Parliament* and amending European electoral laws. But demanding that civil servants be democratically legitimate is utterly grotesque.

The people in the EU bureaucracy are appropriately qualified as a result of their credentials. Back where they come from, they have left a lot behind, things not everyone would be willing to give up 'for a job': family, social cohesion and basically everything you might positively associate with being 'at home'. In contrast to diplomats, however, to whom that could also apply, they are not bound to a *raison d'état* (which, in certain circumstances, could even break a thinking person's back—I, for example, would not have wanted to be an Austrian diplomat when Wolfgang Schüssel, having come in third in the Austrian national election, 'politically legitimated' himself with the help of Jörg Haider and became chancellor in 2000, forming an Austrian government that made a cult out of the Austro-fascist leader Engelbert Dollfuss and, under that canopy, conducted political business now known to the court). The European Commission's civil servants are solely bound to an inherently enlightened rationality. They didn't win their jobs through paternalistic interventions, protections and party memberships, but essentially through education and competency. Every year, between 25,000 and 30,000 people seek civil servant jobs at a European institution, competing in a difficult, three-stage selection process at the end of which perhaps 100 receive a job— 100 out of 30,000! I have to admit, I really admire those who succeed. I wouldn't be able to do it. In spite of my enthusiasm for the European project, I would not have the persistence to prepare for such a test and then take it. But I can attest that the qualifications and qualities of those who succeed differ markedly from the slick lubricity and mopish conformism we see in those whose national careers frequently put them in the public eye.

A civil servant in the European Commission, an Englishman who had previously worked in the Cabinet of the British prime minister, explained to me with a very vivid example the difference between a classical, national bureaucracy and the rationality of the European bureaucracy: 'Whenever we, the prime minister's staff,' he told me, 'discussed a problem and came to a decision, there were about 10 people in the room and we reached an agreement in half an hour. Everyone had the same social pedigree, spoke the same language, attended the same university, and had the same teachers—in other words, the same background. We all, more or less, had the same network that advanced our careers, the same experiences and the same opinions. Our wives came from the same social class and our children attended the same elite schools. But we spent far more time discussing how we could then sell our decision to the media than we ever spent discussing the actual problem. With the Commission, it's exactly the opposite, and that's what makes working here so fascinating and educational. Men and women sit together, each of whom comes from a different country, has a different background, is from a different social class or stratum, has a different first language, has attended a different university, and most of them have partners who have yet another mother tongue and a different background. Our detailed discussions can last for hours, even days. Our discussions draw on many more experiences, have more inputs and are thus more creative. And we never talk about how we can then peddle the results to the media. Because our experience has unfortunately been that, no matter what we do, it ultimately comes down to how the various national media filter things to the public . . . '

In most cases, the oft-maligned Commission's officials demonstrably work much more progressively and rationally than every individual EU member state in and of itself. To cite one example: until recently, employment contracts in Germany were written based on the Civil Law Code of 1923. Just imagine: 1923 as the foundation for labour law at the beginning of the twenty-first century! The Legal Service of the European Commission reviewed the contracts and brought them before the European

Union's Court of Justice* (yes, many bureaucrats were involved!), whose decree, which Germany ultimately had to implement, fundamentally improved the workers' rights and eliminated a number of discriminatory practices that, up until that point, had been legal in German employment contracts.

In the past five years, more than 60 such proceedings, successfully brought before the European Court of Justice by the European Commission, have been conducted against Germany alone. Millions of people benefit from the fact that progressive EU guidelines, regulations and EU Court of Justice verdicts overrule national laws; but then they read or hear that the EU is a bureaucratic monster.

This begs the (as far as I'm concerned, justifiable) question as to what would actually be gained if this enlightened bureaucracy were increasingly subject to traditional, democratically legitimate entities (that is, national governments). If these people were bound to the directives of nationally elected political representatives, if they were dependent upon votes in their home countries, would they let themselves be carried along by the lashes of their national media, which imperiously formulate the desires of national economic and political elites as popular opinion? Would they be dependent upon the short-term interests of the member states' governments, whose horizon reaches as far as the next election date? They would immediately produce, at a minimum, unproductive, if not publicly dangerous contradictions—instead of developing rational regulations undeterred by even the backwardness of large portions of the population of the EU member states along with their resentments and subservient yearning for authoritarian leaders.

(I simply want to put up for discussion my observations and what I've deduced from them. I don't insist on them, and I'm familiar with the objections. I have them myself!)

9

Rampant bureaucracy? Only three European institutions are definitely growing: the Parliament, the Court of Justice and the Court of Auditors. That is to say, democracy, legal certainty and budgetary controls. All the other institutions, as far as the number of bureaucrats is concerned, are numerically stable and spare.

10

Brussels.

Cities have always fascinated me. For a long time, I couldn't fall asleep because I was too busy daydreaming my way into other cities. I thought my life was too small, too restricted, too regimented and insufficiently urban. By the way, I come from Vienna. I studied literary history. For all intents and purposes, I studied 'the history of the narrated city'. Aren't the real protagonists of great novels often cities—Paris, London, New York, St Petersburg and, yes, even (old) Vienna? And aren't the cities the true catalysts for the characters, the source of their misery and their happiness? I didn't want to just *visit* those metropolises; I wanted, as soon as I could, to *live* in them, to make my fortune there. It took some time for me to understand that, for all the cities I had dreamt of, their time had passed. They're museums of their respective histories, theme parks of their clichés, for the development of which perhaps there were good reasons at some point in history.

It's strange how few people realize that there are hardly any widespread international clichés about Brussels. Are you familiar with any? Those that do exist do not refer to Brussels but to 'Brussels', the city in quotation marks as the symbol for EU bureaucracy and its problematic, if not to say, inadmissible claims to interfering in the affairs of European countries. A clichéd perception, in other words, that doesn't owe its existence to a saccharine history but, rather, to a contemporary condition improperly understood. But very few people realize that, for historical reasons, Brussels can now be seen as a prototype of the future European metropolis.

Brussels is the capital of a nation that only belatedly decided to become a nation, and one that never really committed itself to the idea. On what basis should it have done so? A romantic notion of the nation could not emerge from among the three linguistic groups randomly living together on their apportioned territory. The notion of a nation by consent couldn't really develop in a state in which consent consisted of accepting a joint king, provided far-reaching autonomy rights were granted to all parties whose only commonality was the table at which the allocation of the public budget was negotiated. Not even the Flemish nationalists have a common conception of how their nationalism could be effected. Through national sovereignty for Flanders? Through linguistic but not necessarily cultural unification with the Netherlands? Or through cultural but not linguistic affiliation with Germany? Hugo Claus' novel *The Sorrow of Belgium* (1983), the greatest work of Belgian national literature—which consists solely of this one volume—is a textbook study of the grotesque historical dislocations arising from that human disaffection known as nationalism, which currently is growing in Belgium as vigorously as the fingernails of a dead person. That, however, is only a problem for the nationalists, for those zombies from the nineteenth century, that is. For contemporaries, on the other hand, and precisely for that reason, Brussels is the appropriate administrative capital of the European Union—the concrete, animate and vibrant vision of a postnational Europe. In the final analysis, there exists a relaxed, orderly chaos of identities. Multilingualism is such a given in Brussels that it's not the polyglot who is the odd one but the monolingual. The city has 19 mayors. What we consider to be 'Brussels' is, in fact, the 'Brussels region', consisting of 19 cities. Each mayor defends—with increasing helplessness—the sovereignty of his or her incorporated region within the city. There are historical reasons for the system, but it clearly and simultaneously appears as both political folklore and an experimental design for the future. In the city—as if in a laboratory—the problems of the entire continent are being played out. At some point, the European heads of state will discover that the whole will get the better of its constituent parts.

Strolling through the stately Belle Époque streets, you never feel like you're in a museum. Life flows through them; neither tourists nor parvenus rule the pavements. It's as if the city has a collective will that refuses to become a mere facade.

Turning some corners, you're confronted with misery and contemporary distress.

The current austerity policy imposed upon Europe (which truly was not a sovereign decision made in Brussels) can be seen in the fact that no attempt has been made to hide the distress. Groups of homeless people wrapped in blankets, huddled in doorways or around warm heating grates.

And the passers-by: appearing more compassionate than resentful.

II

I began to learn the true nature of the problem with democratic legitimacy in the EU's institutions in May 2010, during the European Council* summit at which the actions in response to the perilously high Greek budget deficit were initially discussed.

To begin with, on 6 May, the eve of the summit, I experienced the following in the serene and elegant Café Cirio in Brussels: five German tourists, fuelled by Belgian stout, had started raucously railing against 'the Greeks'. It grew unpleasant, not only due to the volume but also because of the derogatory clichés they spouted. Brussels is, as I've said earlier, a polyglot city. The waiter goes to the table and says in German: 'Would you like to pay?' One of the Germans: 'No. We don't want to pay yet. We haven't asked for the cheque!' The waiter: 'You can tell them over there in the Council building that you don't want to pay. But here, you need to pay and then please leave.'

That, of course, was not a nationalistic response by the waiter to 'the Germans' and their stomping stereotypes. It was a cool statement about the demonstrative nationalism of the Germans aimed at 'the lazy and corrupt Greeks'. It's worth noting that the waiter, by referring to the Council, related the German tourists' behaviour to Germany's European policies, which, in spring 2010, when I was staying in Brussels, were being discussed everywhere.

Indeed, it's far more than a simple update of a cliché to observe that Germans haven't exhibited so much nationalism in a very long time, an attitude, by the way, that—given the legit-imizing ideologies of the EU and the course of European integration—should increasingly be disappearing. It was and is German politics that, already for months at that particular time (and, less apparent, but in hindsight discernible, for years already, since the end of the Helmut Kohl era), declares European problems to be problems of the nation-states—the Greek state, the Italian state, the Portuguese state, etc. And it's German politics that, completely unperturbed and systemati-cally, turns a European institution, the Council, into a body for defending national interests, especially one's own.

Bringing one's national interests into an alliance of nation-states together with the aspiration of superseding them through a postnational process can be reasonable and necessary. But given such a process, you would then have to discuss what kind of national interests would be meaningful—for instance, the aspiration of not abandoning at that higher level the standards you've already fought for and established within the nation-state governing democratic participation, civil rights, social equality, environmental protection, etc. But that discussion never effectively took place. *Au contraire*, the political and economic elites—above all, the powerful member states—have systematically and repeatedly lowered those very standards to the detriment of their own population, citing the apodictic justification that precisely 'no alternative' is ineluctably necessary for European integration and/or in order to remain 'competitive'.

That was problematic enough (and highly profitable for Germany's industry) but wasn't essentially different from the economic and social policies of some other EU member states. What's really unique and scandalous, however, is how brazenly, and with no sense whatsoever of their own history, German governmental policy in concert with some mass media has constructed the bugaboo of a scapegoat once the European misery—on account of their very policy—became insufferable and could no longer be overlooked. Following the experiences of the first half of the twentieth century; following the shock, the contrition, and the 'Never again!' rhetoric of 1945; and following the decades-long commitment to a united, peaceful, postnational Europe, you wouldn't think it were still possible in today's Germany to create a bogeyman so promptly, so potently and so fanatically that it could unite virtually everyone, from industrialists to the long-term unemployed, in nationalistic hatred to form a *Volksgemeinschaft* (ethnic or racial community), intent on punishing the 'foreign parasites' living on the 'healthy, German *Volkskörper*' (racially pure body politic; when used today, the two terms clearly have National Socialist connotations). It's almost pointless wanting to try to explain that this induces greater fear in me than Greece's debts or the budget deficits in other countries. For anyone who is appalled by Greece's debts and dreads the incalculable consequences they will have on European prosperity and social peace will argue that this particular financial problem is an objective issue and that a different way of thinking about it in Germany will not change anything. On the contrary, given the tough years the German populace endured during the labour market, unemployment and welfare reforms of the early twenty-first century, people have to be more understanding and not rebel against additional payments that are required to rescue another country which didn't manage its economy as well as Germany did.

One could offer a counterargument that . . . —and will hear the objection: yes, but . . . —and so on and so forth. That leads to pendular arguments that soon become esoteric, that is, mere oscillations in which every prognosticator can discern his or her own truth.

But no matter how you interpret the budget deficits of individual EU countries, and regardless of whether you consider the steps taken to deal with the crisis adequate or insufficient, an essential aspect of the problem gets completely ignored in such debates, namely, the fact that the present crisis and the handling of it essentially touch upon the last great taboo— according to their self-understanding—of enlightened democracies. That taboo is democracy itself, the organizational form of democratic legitimacy, and of European politics in particular. The problem clearly manifests itself, providing you're willing to see it, in the structure of the European Union. Taking a closer look at it will cause you to be appalled. Can it be that the democracy we have painstakingly—and by no means ideally—come to know since 1945, the democracy to which we have become accustomed, is incapable of functioning at a supra-national level? Not at all. The democratic legitimacy conferred upon nation-states, however, is completely incapable of solving all the problems and transformational crises of postnational development. Indeed, on a supranational level it is the democratic legitimacy of nation-states that actually creates and continually exacerbates the problems. Doesn't the crisis of the EU arise from the fact that the proponents of national interests 'legitimately' and consistently obstruct pan-European policies so that a 'sovereign' national solution to a problem is no longer possible while a solidary supranational solution cannot be achieved? Taking this into account, the problem would not be the lack of democratic legitimacy within European institutions—the frequently invoked 'democratic deficit' of the EU—but, rather, what we mean by the term 'democratic legitimacy'.

Prior to explaining that, I need to say one thing. Before I came to Brussels, I had some prejudices about the EU. Nothing dramatic, they were just judgements, the natural ambivalences of an attentive newspaper reader who considers himself a critical contemporary. No one, I thought, will question the significance of the idea behind the European project: transcending the historical enmities among the European nation-states and creating enduring peace and freedom on the continent. An idea, however, no matter how great or reasonable, tells you nothing about the organizational form in which it is supposed to develop as completely as possible. It's a fact that all the states that have joined the EU are democratic states. But it's also a fact that, in the process, the democratic standards that had been attained in the nation-states have been lost, if not to say, consciously abandoned, at the supranational level. No one, not even an ardent advocate of the 'European idea', will deny that. Hence my ambivalence, since the European Union attempts to implement a great idea through a system that undermines that idea, causing democracy to dissipate. That process needs to be critically examined. To be sure, the Treaty of Lisbon led to certain improvements over the Maastricht Treaty. But it not only didn't completely eliminate the democratic regressions and deficits, it also carved some of them in stone. Here's one example that seems striking to me: you can only speak of a developed democracy if a separation of powers exists. That's a fundamental component of the notion of democracy as it has progressed since the Enlightenment, an indispensible element in the practice of democracy as it has been fought for or, in the case of Germany and Austria, presented to us. To be sure, the Parliament is an elected body, but it has no authorization to initiate laws—or now, subsequent to Lisbon, only through the back door.

The right to initiate legislation—the right, that is, to propose new legal acts (regulations and directives)—belongs to the European Commission. It also has the right to enforce the laws, though, which is an executive competence. Thus the legislative and executive are conflated within the Commission, a situation that struck me as problematic. The European Parliament is democratically legitimate; its members are elected to perform their functions. The rights and capabilities of the Parliament, however, are curtailed. The European Council, the assembly of the European heads of state, is at least indirectly democratically legitimate, since the heads of state have been elected as the top candidates in their national elections. The Commission, however, is the institution in which democratic legitimacy is ultimately removed. It is an operation that has superseded the separation of powers and is represented by commissioners, who themselves are only doubly indirectly, that is, homeopathically legitimate—dispatched by the nation-states in which, however, they were not elected, and only confirmed by the Parliament but not elected by it. From a democratic perspective, the triad of Parliament, Council and Commission thus produces a black hole into which what we consider to be democracy disappears. I therefore thought that—given all the advances of the European project like disappearing borders, freedom of establishment and a common currency—the basic abolition of democracy was a scandal, and thus a commitment to the European idea would have to take the form of criticizing that scandal.

Then I came to Brussels.

Actually, the democratic legitimacy of the Council is a mere chimera. The heads of state constituting the Council have been elected as the top candidates of the national parties in national elections, but no voter made his or her electoral decision dependent upon which of the national candidates would make the best possible supranational decisions. On the contrary, national interests were delegated to people who, in turn, were expected to represent those—and only those—national interests. To say that the elected representatives of national interests are automatically, as if by magic, co-legitimate whenever they fly to Brussels to also behave like representatives of supranational reason is—to put it mildly—theoretically very generous. Within the Council, the superficially demagogic interests of the voters in the nation-states and the profoundly powerful interests of national economic elites are negotiated, leading to surreal, short-sighted decisions that immediately produce new problems, causing the Council to gather once again in search of solutions. You can definitely see that by looking at Germany's recent European policies. When Germany clearly exceeded the designated limit of 3 per cent for new budget indebtedness in 2005, it arranged—together with France, which likewise was deeper in debt—for easing the terms of the Stability Pact so as to avoid an admonition by the Commission. Once the German budget had been stabilized and the consequences of the relaxed stability regulations were being felt more drastically throughout Europe, Germany responded by demanding the reinstitution of the previous, more stringent regulations.

In 2008, when the Commission analysed the financial crisis that clearly began to loom as a result of Germany's politics, the requisite amount for overcoming the crisis was estimated at 250 to 300 billion euros. The newly implemented criteria (which were not as sweeping as what Germany is now calling for) along with the approved mechanisms to effectively monitor compliance with the criteria would have contained the crisis and prevented its most drastic repercussions. At the time, it would have cost Germany approximately 60 billion. But Germany put its foot down. Partially surrendering its sovereignty to achieve a controlled pan-European fiscal policy was counter to Germany's interests and thus unfeasible. The outcome is readily apparent nowadays—and will cost the Federal Republic of Germany considerably more. But is that sufficient reason to fuel nationalistic resentments against 'the Greeks'?

The Greek deficit amounts to less than 2 per cent of the GNP of the EU. That problem can't find a European solution? The state of California's debt is significantly higher. California is basically bankrupt, along with an array of other US states. The magnitude of the problem is the same as if, in Europe, Germany and France were bankrupt. But nowhere do I read or hear about a panic ensuing that could tear the USA apart. Nowhere do I read suggestions that California should leave the dollar zone. In Europe, though, Greece, an economically utterly insignificant country, is bankrupt and, in all seriousness (or serious stupidity), there are speculations about the end of the euro.

Contrary to the thinking of the Commission and the reservations voiced by almost all the European states, Germany managed to push through the idea that, in order to save the euro, the USA, in the form of the IMF,* should be brought on board—the same IMF, that is, whose conditions and requirements already led a proud and wealthy Argentina into bankruptcy (along with all the repercussions that no one in Europe can seriously want to have: a soaring suicide rate, civil-war-like conditions, etc.). When the German banks suffered, Frau Merkel forked over 400 billion without much ado, but during the European currency's stability crisis—a crisis to which Germany also contributed—for weeks Frau Merkel couldn't bring herself to give her approval to a bailout package that would have cost the 17 European countries 120 billion together. Worse: back home, where she had been elected and where she was facing another regional election in which she feared the rage of the 'German taxpayers', she tried to avoid any mention that the sum involved was a monetary gift to another country, preferring instead to call it a commitment to lend. She thus obstructed an eminently important European political decision on account of a German provincial election, and when the elections in North Rhine-Westphalia were concluded and Frau Merkel's party was ultimately defeated, she linked the aid to Greece with German arms deals in Greece. In other words, she provided assistance that was only profitable for her own export industry and then floated the idea that every country could become the world's leading exporter. What kind of European policy is it that, on the one hand, conducts negotiations with Turkey about the possibility of their joining the EU and, on the other, forces a prostrate EU member state into an expensive arms build-up aimed at Turkey? What kind of European policy is it that cashes in national export profits by arming one NATO member against another? Has the question ever been asked in the German media or among drinking buddies in a German pub whether that policy isn't gaga? If Greece were as corrupt as the German government likes to broadcast in the German media, wouldn't those weapons deals only be able to come about through immense bribery payments? Isn't that why the Greek minister who was responsible for the purchase of

German submarines is now sitting in prison for corruption? It can't be the state's job, though, and certainly not that of the German state, to provide legal compliance for dirty deals.

And so on and always so forth. That is what we can expect from 'democratically legitimate' politics. But the bogeyman of the average German consumer is the 'bloated European bureaucracy' and its 'mania for regulations'. Yes, it proposes regulations—for example, regulating the financial markets. For years now, those are ideas that, whenever the Commission presents them to the Council for discussion, never find their way onto the agenda of the Council summits.

Yesterday, Frau Merkel was absolutely certain that the financial markets didn't need any regulation, as if the slightest intrusion on the speculators' freedom constituted the greatest threat to everyone's freedom. Today, she's certain that some regulation would be necessary. Yesterday, she was certain that the Treaty of Lisbon completely covered the legal capacity of the European Union. The objections of the treaty's critics were ignored and the treaty was democratically rubber-stamped in the Bundestag. Today, however, she's certain that some aspects of the treaty really do need to be changed. Then she was certain that Europe didn't need a common economic, financial or fiscal policy. Moments later, however, she could image a 'European economic cabinet' and common fiscal standards. At the same time, she was certain that the 'economic cabinet' should not involve forsaking national sovereignty, which is why she could only imagine the 'economic cabinet' as a meeting of the national ministers in the European Council. Such a meeting, though, has already been happening for a long time. What she said, then, was: Now it just has a different name. Now, however, she's certain that for a common European budget policy it would be necessary for the states to cede responsibilities and grant controlling capabilities to Europe. 'We need to deepen our political union,' she finally said. The next day, however, she added that one 'shouldn't expect a deepening of our political union quite yet'. Then she was completely certain that the question of whether a country should remain in the eurozone should not be decided by a referendum and she sought the dismissal of Greece's prime minister George Papandreou when he announced such a referendum. Then she was suddenly certain that the best thing for Greece would be to combine a national referendum about remaining in the eurozone with new parliamentary elections there.

How certain can I be about the rationality of what Frau Merkel will certainly know tomorrow? Nevertheless, given the growing problems, she admits, to some extent, to things that, had she accepted them years earlier, would have prevented the ominous escalation of the problems. That's what's called pragmatic politics. But can you really only expect from political pragmatism the management of crises that only assumed the magnitude they did on account of that very pragmatism?

Yes, democracy. It sounds good. It confers legitimacy. But for what purpose? International companies put pressure on national governments to assert their global interests, and the governments turn those interests into national issues (jobs, tax revenues . . .) and thus torpedo the development of solidary supranational politics.

That's the point at which perhaps you have to be willing to admit that it would at present be an improvement, a liberating step, if our social parameters were no longer essentially decided through national elections. You don't even have to recall the depths to which the competition for democratic legitimacy sinks whenever populist parties fight for the votes of xenophobic, racist and authoritarian personalities.

In the Commission, there are no sinister figures, no fascists and anti-Europeans (like those now sitting in the Parliament), no stooping opportunists (like in national governmental organizations) who are not bent by the weight of their responsibilities but by the pressure of the most powerful special interests. In the European bureaucracy, there are no resentful cooks going their own way and disregarding everyone else, no one taking out their anger on others. Maybe there are some cynics—who have experience. There are surely missionaries—who are committed to enlightened causes. Above all, there are true pragmatists—who make use of and expand every opportunity the prevailing distribution of power provides. They all share an enlightened mentality that thinks in transnational categories. They think far ahead, in their recently accepted Agenda 2020 (with deletions made by the Council) and in their 'Groupe de reflexion 2030'. And always with the explicit aspiration of safeguarding and enlarging Europe's social achievements and establishing greater shared economic-political governance.

You should have the civil servants tell you what it's like to be working for years on proposals for overcoming the budget crisis only to have to watch how those proposals are routinely sent back by the heads of state on the Council so that they can then report to their constituents back home about all the things they pushed through to defend their 'national interests' against the 'evil EU' as well as all the things they obstructed in the interests of their constituents. Once the crisis became dramatic, the heads of state charged the Commission to develop 'proposals for solving the financial crisis', that is, for the Commission to keep doing exactly what it had been doing and what the Council kept refusing to put on their summit agendas. To complement the three types of civil servants outlined above, I would add a fourth type: the depressed civil servant. But come evening, the Europeans sit in their cafes and restaurants behind the Berlaymont building, washing away their frustrations with a beer and conversation—and go back to work the next day.

So many conversations. And it was only there, by closely observing the structures and practices of the EU, I realized that classical democracy, a model that developed into a sensible framework for organizing the nation-states in the nineteenth century, could simply not be superimposed upon a supranational union because it would only impede it. Democracy presupposes educated citizens. When, in light of the baiting crowds stirred up by the mass media, educated citizens are no longer in the majority, democracy constitutes a public danger. The EU legitimates itself as a 'peace project' through which the individual states become increasingly intertwined and coalesce. If, however, contrary national interests become institutionalized within the Union and, in the shortest span of time, it becomes possible to foment resentments in one member state against another on the magnitude we have recently seen, then the ideo-logical canopy becomes threadbare—and beneath that canopy the wolves roam freely.

But perhaps the historical ingenuity of reason will once again prevail. With every tiny step wrested from the crisis on the way to a postnational development towards a common solu-tion to the already substantially intertwined problems, the nation-states, and thus the Council as well, become less impor-tant. In the end, the heads of state will politely be requested to leave when the new democracy unfolds, a system of checks and balances between a truly European parliament of regions and the enlightened, Josephinian civil service organization of the Commission.

At any rate, it was too bad Frau Merkel wasn't at the Café Cirio on the eve of the Council summit. She probably wouldn't have had to pay. Monsieur Jean would have ushered her out with the words, 'You are my guest!'

12

The crisis summit of the European Council in March 2010 was for me truly a master class on the so-called democratic legiti-macy of European political decisions. In the days and weeks preceding the summit, it was clear to everyone that the main issues would be finding a solution to the EU's financial crisis as well as that of the EU member state Greece. But Greece was not included on the official agenda of the summit. Why not? Leading up to the summit, Greece was the only topic of discussion. The Commission was dealing with it cross-departmentally. No matter whom I spoke to, they talked about nothing else. None of that activity was particularly productive for my novel, but it certainly constituted a constructive post-graduate political seminar. There was a series of suggestions and discussions from the European Parliament devoted to the topic, and no other European political issue appeared in the media. The experts in the Commission had developed a well-formulated argument for solving the Greek budget problem, presented by the president of the Commission, José Manuel Barroso. It was lying right there on the table. The EU bureaucracy was working transparently. The information was flowing. Things were being discussed. Heads of national governments, however, are apparently used to conducting politics as a game of obfuscation, deflection, private negotiations and tricks. The only agenda item on the summit of the European heads of state was Chile.

Chile!

You might accuse me of naivety, but I was scandalized when the agenda was made public. I thought—and still do think—it was commendable for the European Council to resolve to provide assistance to the earthquake victims in Chile. But the way things transpired, victims on another continent were misused to conceal national disagreements in Europe. If the Council were unable to reach a compromise among German, French and British interests concerning the European financial crisis, then that ultimately wouldn't constitute a 'failure' since the problem wasn't even part of the official agenda. The summit had to be a 'success'—and that success was preordained: 'Resolved: Humanitarian Aid for Chile!' If they should also happen to reach an agreement concerning Greece—the overtly covert summit topic—then they could also point to that great success, one that could only even be considered, however, once the possibility of a failure was precluded from the outset.

But what happened was worse.

I procured journalist credentials and was thus able to enter the Justus Lipsius building, the headquarters of the Council. There the observer is presented with a banal yet rather interesting spectacle. Following an elaborate choreography, the heads of state arrive individually at precise, one-minute intervals, entering the Council building via the red carpet and greeted with a handshake from the Council president's chief of protocol. Some are more communicative and linger a bit in front of the retinue of journalists, say two or three sentences into the microphones or cameras, and then head off with a smile should any journalist actually pose some questions; others simply bustle seriously past the journalists.

It's a vision every child could imagine. Eventually, all 27 of them disappear into a conference room. The journalists gear up for a long wait.

Suddenly, and much too early to seriously think the deliberations have already reached a conclusion, the door of the conference room opens and two heads of state emerge: the German chancellor and the French president. They rush down the corridor and disappear behind another door. And the journalists? With each passing moment, they lose any and all interest in the 'summit'; their attention is fixated on the door behind which Frau Merkel and Monsieur Sarkozy have disappeared.

You have to imagine the scene, as if you had all the time in the world your displeasure affords: 25 political representatives, who have at their political disposal what is so marvellously called 'democratic legitimacy', are sitting in a room and—doing what? Playing cards? Drinking coffee? Exchanging restaurant tips? It doesn't matter. They can do whatever they want. It's irrelevant because the decision, in order that it can even come to one, is being made one door away where an 'institution' is meeting, and institution that is not described, defined or legitimized in any constitution, any European treaty or any democratic substratum—the institution known as 'Merkozy'.

At some point, the door opened again and Frau Merkel, looking stern, and Monsieur Sarkozy, with a crimson face, returned to the summit. Then the summit came to a conclusion. The Council president appeared before the media, announced that 'in an open and very productive discussion, blah, blah, blah . . . ' That was followed by the press conferences of the heads of state. I have to admit, I can't remember if even one sentence about Chile was ever uttered.

A declaration was presented—dictated by German financiers, the German export industry, and in fear of the German taxpayers—and approved by the remaining heads of state, who wanted to spare themselves an embarrassing veto by Frau Merkel as well as a systematic pan-European solution. The economic powerhouse Germany blackmailed the other 26 member states of the EU. Today, we know just how dearly that would come to cost not only the people of Greece and the other EU member states but also Germany itself.

I'm not a journalist. I don't have to pretend to be impartial and balanced, qualities that are actually often driven by 'national pride' or the belief in the legitimacy of 'national interests'. I only describe my impressions and experiences.

'Democratic legitimacy'. In the room where the elected representatives of the states were sitting, without a portfolio for even discussing the proposals of the European Commission and blindly awaiting a 'compromise' from Frau Merkel and Monsieur Sarkozy, 'my' chancellor was also sitting. How legitimate is an institution in which the only person who stood to be democratically elected by me can only state after the summit what Frau Merkel had decided?

13

That's what, for the time being, makes it so difficult to have a discussion in Germany about the democratic development of Europe. The efforts of the Commission, the only truly pan-European institution trying to develop pan-European solutions, are perceived as undemocratic, bureaucratic high-handedness, whereas the considerations, concerns, sentiments and stupidities of a chancellor who would like to be re-elected in Germany are considered in Germany—where she had been *elected* in the first place—to be democratically legitimate as far as European politics are concerned. It is, as a matter of fact, indisputable that the German claim to leadership within the EU is the democratic problem. In 27 of the current 28 member states, Frau Merkel was not elected, could not be elected and would not be elected.

You don't have to draw upon (entirely plausible) psychological interpretations to explain why Angela Merkel can never really become a European politician. Unlike Helmut Kohl, for instance, she, given the year in which she was born, was no longer shaped by the shock of the devastation and crimes committed in the name of German nationalism. Having grown up in the GDR, she experienced such postulates as 'Peace to the people!' and 'No more fascism!' as empty phrases and mantras of self-legitimacy in an unfree state. What were her opportunities in life and her perspectives like? Freedom—what must that have concretely meant for her? As far as I know, she wasn't even allowed to study what she really wanted to. The fact that she nevertheless completed her assigned studies with a grade of 'very good' attests to her dedication and diligence, but as far as dissidence, criticism and political engagement were concerned, she never stood out. Opportunities in life, perspectives, freedom and career possibilities—all those things only really opened up for her following the fall of the Wall. Wouldn't German reunification, the national rebirth of Germany, have to constitute for her the pinnacle of what could be politically and biographically attainable? Can she, who personally owes everything to the national redemption of Germany, understand in the depths of her heart what postnational development really means? So that she can think historically: Must not the punishment for historical German nationalism have consisted in the division of Germany, which is to say that with the disappearance of the GDR the punishment was served, making an innocent and guiltless German nationalism once again possible? Can her socialization visualize different historical goals than the ones that have already been reached and reconfirmed: a united, democratic Germany—along with her re-election? As a citizen of the GDR she wasn't allowed to travel. Wouldn't a passport therefore constitute sufficient proof of the right to freedom of movement? So what can the possibility of travelling in Europe without needing that sacred passport mean to her? Why should she prevent her homeland security minister from reinstituting passport controls in Europe? After all, everyone does have a passport. Can she, who had to live so long without one, see any problem in having to show it?

On account of its biographical imprinting, Kohl's generation had a better idea of what the European project is all about. The generation after Merkel, the Erasmus generation, knows it even better, and also differently, as a result of their concrete experiences with European achievements. But Merkel's era constitutes the interim period on the path between a Europe of reconciliatory nations and a borderless, solidary and postnational Europe, an interim period in which Germany once again seeks favour as a great and powerful nation. National pride, however, can never completely be had without resentments and aggressions directed at others . . .

Of course, the crisis in which the European project now finds itself cannot simply be reduced to the human factor, to the socialization and imprinting of Europe's current leaders. Indeed, the cracking and crashing currently occurring in

Europe's foundations are the logical consequences of the Union's structural defects and not just the results of the behaviour of its political personnel.

14

The structural defect lies in the fact that the nations, whose power is supposed to be diminishing, must at the same time command sufficient power since it is the very representatives of the nations that must come together to transcend the nations. If we think back to the beginning, we see that those were precisely the steps that were taken. To initiate postnational development and establish supranational institutions, the national governments first had to jointly resolve to do just that. Only the governments of sovereign democratic states had the legitimacy to cede or mutualize their sovereignty rights. To accomplish that, a public authority had to be created where the democratically legitimate representatives of the nation-states could meet and, adhering to the rules and procedures of their national parliaments, make their joint decisions. That institution is the European Council. The Council is where the member states' heads of government along with the heads of their respetive departments come together and—theoretically—find and expand their common interests.

With the European Commission and the European Parliament two truly supranational institutions were created for the purpose of advancing postnational development. The Commission develops pan-European proposals, proposes guidelines and ordinances for the entire Union and, as 'guardian of the Treaties', ensures that each member country is properly applying EU law. The Parliament, in turn, whose members are directly elected, controls the Commission, must approve the commissioners' appointments and has the power to unseat them. The Parliament also adopts the EU's annual budget and is the institution charged with safeguarding the democratic legitimacy of all joint decisions. At first, the European Parliament was substantially powerless, but with each new EU treaty and the successive ceding of national sovereignty rights to the community, the rights and possibilities of the European Parliament have expanded.

Inserted between these two supranational institutions, which are truly European in their aspirations and duties, is the Council. Given the structure, the Council has little chance of being anything but a bulwark in defence of national interests. And there are always some national interests that conflict with the pan-European proposals the Commission has developed and the Parliament would like to enact. Those national interests may be mere chimeras or, as the interests of some small, particular groups, contrary to the interest of the majority, or even contrary to any objective logic. But no matter what, those interests clearly represent one thing: the political life insurance of the heads of state, who, elected solely in their respective nation-states, can only guarantee their endorsement and re-election there. And those heads of state can only hope (or, at a minimum, even think about) being re-elected if they can demonstrate to their constituents back home how systematically they defend those interests against any and all others, how they fend off the Union's unreasonable demands, and how they averted any further erosion of their national sovereignty.

The Council, which was established to initiate Europe's communitarization and advance it step by step until the Council itself would became superfluous, has become instead the stronghold of the heads of state and the instrument by which they obstruct the very process they were created to complete. It is therefore not the case that the triad of Commission, Council and Parliament create a black hole into which what we understand to be democracy disappears. The reverse, in fact, is the case. What we understand to be democracy, that is, the purely national legitimacy of political elites, produces a black hole into which the idea and rationale of the European project disappears. Accordingly, that idea and rationale cannot claim democratic legitimacy on a European level and the process through which they disappear is never questioned or subjected to serious democratic debate.

The advent of the so-called financial crisis illustrates that with vivid clarity. It's not necessary to provide a detailed explanation to say at the outset that the majority of the Greek population surely didn't want that crisis. Nor did a majority of the eurozone countries want it. No member state of the EU developed a mass movement that would have created the political pressure to precipitate the turmoil. So what led to the crisis no one wanted? It certainly didn't occur on its own. It was the product of dynamics arising from political decisions. The institutionalized processes by which such decisions come into existence are called 'the system'. The system that produced the crisis is precisely the institutional structure of the European

Union: a poorly balanced relationship between supranational institutions (the Commission and the Parliament) and an institution in which national interests, national sensitivities, national fictions, etc. are defended (the Council). As the adoption of a common European currency was being prepared, it was completely obvious that a common currency requires a common economic, financial and fiscal policy as well as a central bank with all the rights of a central bank—that is, not only having the authority to design bank notes and coins but also having the power to implement monetary policy capable of counteracting crisis-laden developments.

The Commission had drawn up the appropriate proposals. The Parliament would have passed the necessary legislation with large majorities. The Commission as well as the Parliament had thus represented the objective interests of the European populace, that is, their natural desire to have a stable currency. But the European Council would not make common cause with them. The Council thwarted logic and rationality in a wretched game of national affectations and so-called interests, borne on the backs of all those people on the continent and, indeed, the world, who do not happen to be speculators. The Council could agree on a common currency. The French president wanted to be able to proclaim back home that he was able to impede Germany's economic supremacy—which was somehow impending as a result of reunification—by having the Germans relinquish their powerful D-mark and toe the line with a common currency. The German chancellor wanted to declare back home that he had pushed through German reunification, made Germany's national rebirth possible and that the euro would be nothing more than a rechristened mark, controlled by a central bank modelled on the German one. The heads of state of the remaining members participating in the common currency were provided with arguments they could effectively sell in their respective home countries: advantages for exports, the end of exchange rates and their fluctuations within the inter-European market and so on.

The Council thereby ended the commonality of completely different national interests. The true prerequisite for introducing a common currency was obstructed: a common economic, financial and fiscal policy. With Frankfurt, the Germans have a powerful financial market, which doesn't have any interest in being controlled and regulated externally—'by Brussels'—through a European financial policy. The British prime minister understood that very well since he had similar 'national interests', namely, the financial market—City of London. Why should that come under the control of Brussels when 60 per cent of the United Kingdom's gross domestic product (GDP) is generated in London through wild speculation? Moreover, the UK isn't even part of the eurozone. The British prime minister, however, liked the fact that Germany had to abandon its mark. To be sure, the French would have supported European financial governance, but, as the then German finance minister Theo Waigel candidly likes to say today, 'We (the Germans) didn't want the French to have any influence over the central bank.' Of course, national myths play a role here—for example, the Germans' *idée fixe* that all financial policy must be subordinate to battling inflation because inflation leads to Hitler. The fact that, historically, an austerity policy—which helped to make

Hitler possible in the first place—lay between Germany's hyper-inflation, and the Hitler years cannot undermine the German fiscal-political myth, nor can, for instance, the fact that the American Fed is continuously printing money yet the inflation of the dollar is below that of the euro. A press for banknotes: for the Germans, that's a machine that, when you insert paper into it, spits out Hitler. That's why only Germans are allowed to be near such a machine, to make sure it never gets turned on.

That's one way to parse it. At any rate, no matter how you evaluate the individual parts, and no matter what information you have at your disposal or which rumours you believe in, in the end, the objective result was as follows: a common currency was decided upon, but the Council refused to provide the necessary foundation for that common currency.

I'm of the opinion that a common currency is an important and rational step in the further integration of the European project. Or at least it could be. But all the painful experiences we currently have with our currency—the crisis, the enormous costs, the destruction of the quality of life of millions of people, the obliteration of opportunities, the abolition of the ability to plan securely (earnings, pensions), the destruction of social networks—for all that we, along with the majority of the people affected, have to thank the elected representatives and their national interests in the European Council.

A common European financial policy was not possible with Germany. Such a policy would have contradicted the German constitution. As long as the European Parliament remains a body that is not fully endowed with all parliamentary rights, the German Bundestag is prohibited from relinquishing to that Parliament its budgetary sovereignty. But no one has prohibited Germany from consenting to turn the European Parliament into a true parliament. As a matter of fact, with the Treaty of Lisbon—and with massive influence exerted by Germany—the Parliament has been somewhat strengthened, but still has not been fully endowed with all parliamentary rights. In exchange, the power of the Council has increased immensely. The Commission, which, according to the original proposal, was intended to become the government of a unified Europe, has been degraded to a glorified secretary's office for the invigorated Council. The weakening of the Commission and the strengthening of the Council were the Treaty of Lisbon's original sin. The nationalists' gentle putsch was hidden behind the enhancement of the Parliament, which, prior to the treaty's ratification, was proudly put on display. It looked good. It sounded good. But it was so moderate that any additional necessary transfer of sovereignty to Brussels would *have* to be blocked by a decree of the German Federal Constitutional Court in Karlsruhe since, in contrast to the German parliament, the European Parliament is not a 'full-fledged' one.

Since the Council deemed a common European financial, economic and fiscal policy unfeasible at the time the euro was introduced—even though the warnings could not be ignored—the Council came up with the following 'compromise' (which quickly succumbed to cackling laughter): the eurozone states commit to a 'Stability Pact', which is basically a nice declaration of intent. As long as everyone remains well behaved, everything will be fine. The first countries unable to meet the criteria of the 'Stability Pact' were Germany and France.

15

So now Europe looks anxiously at those who, as a result of their policies, caused the crisis and animatedly discusses how they will solve the crisis. All the while, they still consider the perpetrators of the crisis to be the sole legitimate entity to solve the crisis, getting caught up in resentments toward the victims of the crisis and demanding from the perpetrators of the crisis a harsh hand directed at its victims.

There will never be any uprising against the lunacy as long as they can console the victims at home with imperious national pride, telling them others bear all the blame—scapegoats, parasites and those who have been living above their means 'with our money'.

I cannot understand that German teachers, German taxi drivers, German business employees, German civil servants and so on are not in solidarity with Greek teachers, taxi drivers and so on, who, facing the same level of prices and the same high costs of living, only earn a third of what the Germans earn and, in addition, are now expected to forego between 20 to 55 per cent of their income due to an austerity policy reminiscent of the one Heinrich Brüning* instituted, the consequences of which the Germans, of all people, should be well aware. I cannot understand that in Germany there is no public criticism of German 'economic experts' who impose upon Greek employees a reduction in the private sector minimum wage, even though that changes absolutely nothing in terms of state spending. And I cannot understand why in Germany, and only in Germany, there is no public outcry over the fact that German pharmaceutical companies have stopped delivering medications to Greece until they can be certain that the Greek populace votes for the 'right' government.

The majority of Germans prefer to have solidarity with their financial market. They have solidarity with the spectre of 'national interests', the defence of which leads to their own immiseration.

When the epitome of a serious newspaper, the weekly *Die Zeit* (which, ever since my student days, served as my intelligent and loyal companion), prints a headline in huge letters that looks and reads more like that of a tabloid—'EVERYONE WANTS OUR MONEY!'—then it becomes stridently obvious just how far up the creek we are without a paddle.

16

How can you dispose of a construct that was inevitable and necessary but only intended to be temporary, one that can only be abolished if the involved parties agree to it? As long as the Union consists of 28 nation-states, every one of them must have a voice in it. At a certain point in postnational development, however, those voices in the Council representing the nation-states' interests disrupt the rational and desired processes the Commission strives to promote.

Neoliberals do not sit on the Commission or, at least, they do not hold the power there to assert their view of the world. Neoliberal influences, though, do enter via the nation-states' interests. If you sit back and think about it, it's completely crazy: through privatizations, dismantling the welfare state and reducing essential state functions, the nation-states systematically diminish the power of the state. And yet, where the nation-states are supposed to be sensibly dismantled—in the European Community, that is—the representatives of the nation-states insist on wielding a heavy hand.

'Reducing the state' would logically mean more Europe instead of the destruction of both the state and Europe.

17

The problem is therefore the European Council—the purported democratically legitimate and collaborative institution that, however, has not taken democracy to a new level but, rather, nationalism. The Council thus ensures that not only the collective but also each individual member state acquires its share of problems that cannot be solved through the democratic apparatus available to us.

To discuss that, to even think about broaching the topic with the present politically enraged citizens, (still) seems futile as long as 'national sentiments' constitute a basic component of their identity—even though they would indignantly reject being called 'nationalists'.

There are all kinds of notions about what a 'nation' is. The most contradictory feelings and fantasies, the details of which would not necessarily withstand rigorous scrutiny. Hence, there is no universally valid definition of the term 'nation'. The only verifiable facts about the concept are that it is historically so young it can hardly be considered an ontological human need and that, over the course of time, it has produced the greatest historical disasters.

Now please imagine the following: A German, an Austrian and someone from France are talking to one another and the concept 'nation' comes up. Everyone nods. They all think they immediately know what it means. And yet, each one undoubtedly understands something quite different. Should the conversation then turn to the 'EU', a dispute immediately ensues. There is no mutual nodding, and each person understands, expects or fears something else. It's grotesque, isn't it? 'Nation' is an abstraction, which everyone believes to understand concretely; the 'EU' is a concrete project that everyone perceives to be completely abstract. Even the most distinguished German intellectuals and the latest French philosophers are, in their respective flights of fancy, not immune to frequently landing in the depths of their neighbourhood pubs and refuelling there. If that is consistently—and contrary to all experiences—on your mind, then for politicians, whose jobs depend on national elections, it is especially dangerous to publicly shout out, 'Forget that nationalist, pseudo-intellectual babble! We're building rational social parameters for our life together in the EU!' But even though I realize that, I still despise them for their cowardice, which is more than cowardly. It's homicidally stupid. For whoever supports nationalism—'because that's just the way people are'—will be swept away by nationalism, because in the European Union and the globalized world, national furore can never really be satisfied. And the rage will become extreme once people realize that the 'defence of national interests' was a fraud from the get-go. The only things being defended are the interests of the national political and economic elites.

18

Yes, the rage.

No one has yet adequately described how a tautology, a simple semantic doubling, can become the precondition for collective schizophrenia. The slogan 'Europe should belong to its citizens' as the battle cry for a bourgeois Europe presents just such a case. Ever since the end of the partitioning of Europe, and especially since the enlargements of the EU in 2004 and 2007, there is no longer any country in all of Europe that, in terms of its political organization, economic system and society, cannot be considered bourgeois—in the sense of a capitalist economy coupled with democracy and the rule of law.

So how are we to understand the tempest in a teapot accompanying the demand to turn a bourgeois Europe into a 'Europe belonging to its (bourgeois) citizens'? How are we to understand the agitated foot stomping—plastered all over the media—of the 'enraged' and 'courageous' citizens? I want to be me, but I'm someone else? I'm not only stronger than I am, but can't I also confirm through intolerance what I've always legitimized through tolerance? At the time in which 'bourgeois citizen' still had a clear meaning, it didn't require an additional modifier to be effective in social discourse. 'Enraged bourgeois citizens' would be a *contradictio in adjecto*; 'courageous bourgeois citizens', a tautology. The concept 'bourgeois citizen' was complex but still clear. It was complex because it could be defined in many ways—sociologically, economically, politically, legally and morally. And it was clear because by bringing those components together it acquired a precise meaning. The concept 'bourgeois' included a claim to self-interest, which was understood as legitimate—providing it promoted the common good as well, no matter how dialectically. 'Bourgeois' was thus always a social concept, even though it never intended to eliminate unsocial elements. It did, however, oppose asocial elements, who, in the eyes of the bourgeois citizen, were not only criminals and those averse to working but also aristocrats, whose aristocracy was defined not by social utility and ethics but by birth. Equality belonged to the *mise en scène* of bourgeois laws; the misery nomologically arising from the inequality of human talents and possibilities was to be relegated offstage, though. The concept 'bourgeois' thus signified an ideal in which the not-ideal also had its place, thereby legitimizing the misery the bourgeois world itself started producing as a natural part of that ideal. The dedication to the ideal—along with the simultaneous acceptance of an anything but ideal reality—turned the idea of the 'bourgeois world' into a concrete utopia that knows no other future. That constitutes its success as well as its undoing.

'Rage' is thus antibourgeois. What should bourgeois citizens—to the extent they are ones—be enraged about? Social misery? Bourgeois citizens acknowledged that long ago—and know they don't want to be part of it. Enraged about the system? It's their system. They pay their taxes, knowing the state has all the means at its disposal to defend that system, even, if need be, with means contrary to other bourgeois ideals. When citizens want security, they'll agree to restrict their freedom. When they want freedom, they'll forget about brotherhood. When they want brotherhood, then they'll exchange the cold security of the legal system for the florid world of the private sphere. There they'll grumble about the public sphere and so on. And when—in the rifts between the two spheres, in the perpetual failure of bourgeois existence—the kind of disaffection arises that could be described as rage, then bourgeois law has always protected it under the banner of 'freedom of expression'. Its holding cell is the neighbourhood pub where it's demonstrably evident that rage is simply a euphemism for resentment.

And 'courageous'? How courageous do you have to be to use those defined and designated forms of bourgeois protest— freedom of assembly and freedom of speech—in a bourgeois constitutional state? Just that dab of courage you want to cool down. Back when the concept 'bourgeois citizen' still meant something, courage was hardly a given—in the struggle against despotism, in committing one's life to implementing civil rights and in aspiring to develop one's individuality in opposition to the social environment and the spirit of the times. Once their heroic age passed, bourgeois citizens have failed on those fronts. Not only during the dark times of bourgeois history did they lose the struggle against despotism, even in less dark times they legitimized despotism through tolerance. Defending civil rights didn't usually appear to be as profitable to them as exchanging those rights for securities, privileges and snobbery. And the idea of individuality as a social aspiration with an attending profit has been sacrificed to the marketplace where the masses have been uniformed with individual particles. You don't have to understand that, but you do have to be able to afford it.

If the concept 'courageous citizens' constitutes a tautology, then 'enraged citizens' is repugnancy in action. They clench their fists, which are empty because they gave with the hand with which they now think they're going to rebel. They demand political participation while they disdain politics. They demand rationality and elect those who cater to their resentments. They fight against politics where they perceive politics to be—locally, that is (due to a train station, a tunnel or an airport runway)— and then vote for the politics defending their 'national interests', incapable of articulating what they are supposed to be. What interests can they have that are fundamentally different from those of another nation's citizens? The only clear thing is that 'national interests' must be something very different from—perhaps almost opposite to—regional or local interests, which would make for a very interesting realization if the enraged and courageous citizens actually had them. It would, you see, entail self-recognition of the schizophrenia encapsulated in tautologizing the concept. The schism of 'I am someone else' implied in the demand that 'Europe should belong to its citizens' is tantamount to 'Europe, those are the others!' And that, in fact, is precisely the disunity of the citizens who, each in their respective concrete place, live with all their civil rights on a continent that is entirely bourgeois. 'Europe'—that's too distant, too abstract. Its citizens don't see and hear what's being built there. They don't know the responsible agents. Its citizens assume those people have privileges that they themselves would avail of if they ever had the chance to do so, and that enrages them. At the local level, however, they suffer from the opposite malady. Everything is too close for them. They see and hear everything that's being built, and that disturbs them to a certain extent as neighbours. They know the political representatives. They incessantly hear the empty phrases with which they try to placate everyone. They don't see the laws but the empty phrases as a helpless attempt to try to legitimate arbitrariness and profligacy. And that enrages them. Thus the bourgeois world decomposes for its citizens into two parts: one that is too distant and one that is too close. Both are concrete, and the citizens stand in concrete opposition to both of them. Concrete parameters are being produced there, and concrete social conditions here, based on a systematic political logic that you can criticize for many reasons, but not, however, because it is not bourgeois.

If the political organization of bourgeois Europe is not to the European citizens' liking, and if the citizens' possibilities for political participation where they live engender enraged citizens, then there can be two reasons for that. Either (1) Europe—at the respective local levels as well as at the collective supranational level—has betrayed the principles of bourgeois politics and economics. That, of course, is a grotesque thesis and can be immediately refuted. Or (2) the enraged citizens of bourgeois Europe no longer know what the concept 'bourgeois' means, which would be an interesting point indeed. At any rate, in order for the enraged and courageous citizens to overcome their divisiveness, they need a third thing—a kind of glue—to cement their identity. That third thing must lie in the middle, between what's too distant and what's too close. And it must be extremely slimy and sticky. And it also needs to be so abstract that no concrete experience can call it into question. That third thing is the national. It embeds the place where one lives into something larger and greater, which is also not as distant as 'Europe'. It imparts a sense of belonging so abstract it can create a sense of community even where there are concrete differences and boundaries but also objective commonalities.

National identity, a sordid ideology that routinely has led to wars and crimes against humanity, had, at the dawn of the bourgeois era, a single historical rationale: to turn a Europe splintered into innumerable small states, principalities and sovereign provinces into less splintered internal markets, binding together smaller enemies into larger powers that could then protect free trade within their enlarged territorial borders. As disastrous as that concept has proved to be throughout history, it essentially was a historical compromise in terms of the bourgeois interests the European Union is currently implementing as a peace project: a larger market, uniform parameters and legal protection. But instead of seeing bourgeois Europe as the completion of that for which the nation-state was merely a poor and partial solution, the enraged and courageous citizens— now more than ever enveloped in the ideological costume of nationalism, in the murderous masquerade of their ideals— claim to experience themselves as authentic while seeing nothing but deceit in the concrete realization of their history's rationales. Likewise, in their own participation in Europe's embourgeoisement, they see only disenfranchisement and exploitation. Disenfranchisement and exploitation may well be rooted in concrete reality, but as unlikely as they are to be resolved in the retro-chic of nationalism, the enraged and courageous citizens are just as unlikely to recognize their causes in the ambigram of their schizophrenic existence.

The phenomenon of the enraged and courageous citizens might be more differentiated, but empirically verifiable is the fact that they themselves obliterate every internal differentiation whenever they can so as not to divide the movement. Consequently, its demonstrated rage and purported courage neither coincide with bourgeois interests nor do they offer an alternative to bourgeois society, which fundamentally would like to challenge what they see as the purpose of their protest. They're rebelling against their own political representation, which, at the same time, they legitimize nationally. Some day, they'll really need courage—when they look in the mirror.

19

I was born in Austria, into a republic that, following all the devastation and crimes that nationalism and national conflicts had produced over the course of the previous half-century, resolved to learn from its history and become a nation itself. Prior to that, there had been a swarm of nationalisms and supernationalisms. The generation that established the Second Austrian Republic after 1945—and imposed a national identity upon it so belatedly—had, in the course of its lifetime, already lived in four different Austrias with four different political systems and four different identities within shifting territorial borders:

the Austria of the Habsburg Monarchy, the First Republic of German-Austria, the Austro-fascist Ständestaat and the National Socialist Ostmark. Then, the fifth Austria in the life-time of that single generation was established: the Austria of the Second Republic. Who can attest that precisely that fifth Austria should now constitute the realization and felicitous objectification of the 'idea of an Austrian nation'? What is that idea supposed to consist of? How is it supposed to manifest itself? What is the exclusive common bond in the national pride of, for example, people living in the western province of Vorarlberg, Austria—who voted in a referendum to join Switzerland and also voted against the Nazi Anschluss of Vorarlberg—and the residents of the eastern Austrian province of Burgenland, whose capital along with half of its territory was ceded to Hungary?

Austria would most of all prefer to be a 'cultural nation'. That would best suit its tourist industry, although, in the course of developing into a nation after 1945, that idea couldn't be aggressively asserted since it was imperative to maintain Austria's independence—especially vis-à-vis Germany—and, by disassociating Austria from German culture and German language, to be reminded of Austria's state sovereignty.

A 'nation of consent'? God forbid! The Jews were finally gone, and if Austria were to declare itself a nation of consent à la revolutionary France, then anyone could just come along and . . . (Post-fascist Austria, which fervently went about constructing national consciousness after 1945, demanded from those Austrians who did succeed in escaping from Hitler and then wanted to return character references with which they had to verify that they hadn't done anything wrong while they were in exile. Such demands were one of the reasons why many Austrians chose not to return.)

I don't know exactly how it was possible, but it was a masterful achievement. In the course of a few years, almost 90 per cent of Austrians responded affirmatively to a survey that asked whether Austria is a nation. (As far as I know, Austria is the only country that routinely uses surveys to monitor whether its citizens think they belong in a nation. The results are then published as newspaper headlines.) As to the reason for their positive answer, the absolute majority declared: 'Because of its beautiful landscape!'

I think it's good that an increasing number of Germans take advantage of the opportunity—afforded by the freedom of establishment—to come to Austria to study or work. In Austria, they can learn what apparently is so difficult for them to discover at home: how grotesque what we call national identity really is.

National identity, however, should not be confused with mentality. It's not differences in mentalities that lead to different national identities and thus to boundaries. History has shown it's the other way around. If differing mentalities could, or even would have to, resist being subsumed under the abstraction national identity, then the GDR never would have been able to be unified with the FRG. Besides, mentalities develop within regions, independent of national borders. The mentalities in the mountains of Tyrol differ from those in the vineyards of Lower Austria.

Europe, in point of fact, is a Europe of regions. The task of European politics should therefore be to systematically recognize and develop what Europe, in fact, already is.

20

Perhaps I would think differently, at least a bit differently, if Austria had taught me a different lesson, and if, after all its experiences in the first half of the twentieth century, Austria would have justified its belatedly becoming a nation with a call to establish an exemplary democracy, a free and open society on the territory allocated to it, with the structures and means of production bestowed upon it.

It's true, of course—and you can't overstate their value—that civilizing and constitutional standards were developed after 1945 that hadn't existed before. But early on the decision was made—and that decision became the *raison d'état*—not to take the democracy that was given to us completely seriously, to not even fulfil the minimal standards in anything but fragmentary ways. Yes, there are elections. But it's common knowledge that they alone do not constitute sufficient proof of a lively and functioning democracy. The fact that there's a government and, at the same time, a recognized paragovernment, that is, the institutionalized social partnership which was never elected by anyone, and yet the majority of the population confers greater rationality on it than on the constitutional government; that laws are not made by the parliament; that there's a constitution not worth the paper it's printed on because, in addition to it, there's a so-called real constitution, which essentially consists of common law accepted by our elected representatives as authoritative, and which, for example, has repeatedly led to laws that contradict the constitution being turned into constitutional laws by a two-thirds majority, depriving the Constitutional Court of the opportunity to overturn them and, even though they constitute a contradiction to the constitution within the constitution, they are sacrosanct—and so on and so forth. Such things don't disturb anyone. They haven't caused enraged citizens to rebel, as long as prosperity has continued to grow. That indicates that all the expectations for democracy are satisfied by a belief in eternal growth, a claim that has never been considered fundamental to any theory of democracy I'm familiar with.

That's why there's something equally ridiculous and comforting about the fact that, as a result of the crisis in the EU, there's been such vehement criticism of its democratic deficit. That criticism is ridiculous insofar as it generally proceeds from the odd notion that, previously, democracy in the nation-states had been realized in nothing less than an ideal form and that, only now, by relinquishing national sovereignty rights to 'Brussels', has it been destroyed and disappeared. But it's comforting that democracy and the question as to how it should be organized are finally being discussed. That's a discussion about the future. But that discussion will necessarily lead to decisions, which—and that's where the ridiculous and the comforting become sublated in an intricate dialectic—in the gradual approach towards true European democracy, are not supported by the majority.

21

The 1957 Treaty establishing the European Economic Community* codified its 'four freedoms' as the foundation of the
community. That was idealistically significant (in the sense of
classical bourgeois ideals) and, at the same time, also a refer-
ence to the 1941 speech by President Franklin D. Roosevelt to
the US Congress in which he justified the necessity for an anti-
Hitler coalition. At that point in time, Austria, from a political
and democratic point of view, was in the New Stone Age.
People understood 'freedom' merely as 'freedom from the lib-
erators (the Allies)' and a heroic 'anti-Hitler coalition' as essentially the alliance between the Austro-fascist Ständestaat and
Mussolini's fascist Italy.

When Austria acceded to the EU in 1995, people there
were also fired up by ideals, even if they were, in part, childish
and nostalgic ones: a long-standing yearning to merge into a
greater connectedness or the dream of once again having a
say in the former Crown lands. The accession was also associ-
ated with pragmatic hopes, particularly for greater security in
a rapidly changing world and, if nothing else, for safeguarding
the prosperity that had already been attained. After 40 years of
freedom (in a form of capitalism) and democracy, people in
Austria hadn't properly learnt what either capitalism or democracy really meant. But they do seem to have mastered one
thing: a culture of compromise that ensures that all contradictions disappear behind the padded doors of imperial buildings,
never to be seen again. That trait seemed to make Austria particularly well suited for the EU. The democratic deficits of the
EU and the provisional compromises between the interests of

nation-state democracies and their suspension in supranational structures have never engaged the political elites or the public sphere in Austria. But precisely at that time, the ideals of the European community along with the hopes and habits of Austria were dealt their greatest blow. Following the collapse of the Stalinist systems, the dream of a pure, unadulterated free market with a free circulation of capital was reanimated. Capitalism now saw itself as having no opponents, as if the end of the Soviet Union had caused all the social antagonisms and contradictions throughout the world to disappear. The 'four freedoms' degenerated into the legitimizing ideology of neoliberal adventurers and speculators, for whom hardship always means the hardship of others and hence presents no real alternative. Having 'no alternatives'—and accepting that under the heading of 'pragmatism'—became the watchwords of a despicable decade, the carrot animating a whole horde of jackasses. Unfortunately, those jackasses were democratically legitimate politicians. Having attained the highest level of societal wealth ever produced in history, the social accomplishments of the past half-century suddenly couldn't pass muster with businessmen and managers and were accordingly dismantled. Meanwhile, private wealth, the magnitude of which had never before been seen, became concentrated in the hands of an increasingly smaller few. And where was the wrath of the impoverished directed? Towards the poorest of the poor. The hatred of the deceived? Towards those most threatened. The rage of the estranged? Towards strangers. The resentments of those wanting to escape reality? Towards refugees. The outlet for those suffering from an inferiority complex? Persecuting minorities.

We know all that from history. It led to the catastrophes subsequent to which those who had so inhumanely and dicta-torially bellowed then sheepishly stammered 'Never again!' It led to the Montanunion in 1951, to the Treaty establishing the European Economic Community in 1957, and, ultimately, to the EU. Are we now thrown back before the beginning? If the EU didn't exist, if the wolves and the politics of those who, in the individual nation-states, dissemble with the wolves were solely responsible for the continent's future, then we'd have to fear that. But in the meantime, the EU's political system (and that's the best thing that can be said about the status quo) has become so developed that neither the cravings of predatory capitalism, which wants to be mistaken for the freedom to conduct busi-ness, nor the predatory cravings of public anger, which claims to be democratically legitimate, have free range. Of course, peo-ple can—and, indeed, must—criticize the democratic deficits of the construct, but then people also have to be clear about the concept of democracy. The defence of democracy as a nine-teenth-century construct—that is, the nation-state—only exac-erbates the contradictions unproductively.

The much-maligned EU bureaucracy illustrates how an organization liberated from the constraints of short-term thinking can develop sensible solutions. That, of course, was the thinking behind lifelong employment for civil servants: freeing them from the shifting power constellations of govern-ments so that they can keep society's well-being in mind far beyond a given legislative period. The EU Commission very fre-quently does just that. What those highly qualified, enlightened and rational people devise is subsequently destroyed by the provincial defenders of the nation-state because they only think about what they can successfully sell to their constituents: for example, what they advantageously extracted, 'solely for them alone', from the EU at the expense of others. Since nation-state democracies cannot do otherwise, important topics—for example, social policies, taxes, asylum, migration and the minimum wage—do not advance to the level of the EU; they become bargaining chips in the conflicts between nation-states. 'The EU', however, cannot do anything about that. The Commission's officials would agree to uniform tax, social and migration policies. The national, provincial politicians, though, do not allow them because they want to hold on to those topics as collateral against ceding power to the EU and also because they want to keep demagogic-populistic pseudo-solutions as opiates for their constituents. It's not an allegedly aloof civil service apparatus but, rather, the nation-state democracies that obstruct the democratization of the EU. That would pull the rug out from under the provincial politicians' feet. Therein lies the true drama of the EU: that civil servants represent civil society and rationality but 'democracy' is represented by those who must obstruct sensible solutions in order to capture democratic legitimacy. The problem of the EU is that, as far as supranational solutions are concerned, it has too little—not too much—competence, and the fault lies with those we can elect: the national governments.

You would think that the decades-long serendipitous culture of compromise (which is downright exemplary in Austria) would necessarily lead to complicated compromises becoming self-evident at the EU level. As a matter of fact, the outbreak of national resentments and the fury over compromises there highlight the true challenge: the need to interpret the concept of democracy anew and dispose of its nation-state manifestations in the hazardous waste dump of history.

Subsequent to the expulsion from Paradise, its back entrance has not been found anywhere in the world. Everything, therefore, is worth being criticized. But as long as that's the case, people should recognize one thing: the EU is the coolest of all hells on earth.

22

The overdue debate about how the European project could be democratized and what shape postnational development should ultimately assume has been derailed thus far because 'democracy' for most people is still experienced and understood as national democracy, which means that 'democratization' for them can only signify more participatory democracy within the confines of a national democracy. The debate also fails to progress because even those who criticize the democratic deficit of the EU usually don't even consider the EU as capable of being democratized. If anything, they think that 'democratic engagement' could only manifest itself in opposition to the EU. The EU is conceived to be a corporate project and a capitalist project. Didn't Europe's communitarization begin as an economic project, as an economic community? Wasn't a single European market only profitable for restlessly mobile capital, the very mobility of which placed increased pressures upon the workers in national labour markets?

I don't want to get into a discussion here about the naivety of thinking it's possible to somehow domesticate international capital solely through national democratic engagement—and its standing in quirky contradiction to the pride many (particularly in Germany) feel towards their own national corporations, which themselves have long been searching for world markets—and to the pride in the 'workmanship' of those corporations whose products carry a designation of origin from their own country, and to the pride in their workplace in those very corporations and so forth. I don't want to remind the Left of Karl Marx's principle that the economy is the basis, and I don't want to remind the Right that they all nodded vigorously to the sentence, 'It's the economy, stupid!' It's interesting that under the anti-capitalist rainbow, 'culture' suddenly appears, and in duplicate form, no less: as deficit and as arrogation.

The deficit: whenever the EU is criticized as a Europe of corporations and capital, then, in that context, there's suddenly no more talk about democratic deficits but, rather, the lack of a unifying idea, a common culture and a cultural identity. No one approaches it at the superstructural level—but Europe, of course, has to consist of more than just a marketplace for capital, a Moloch in the interest of cold, capitalist logic caught in the grip of lobbyists. At the same time, the argument is immediately put forward that there can be no such thing as a common idea, a common culture unifying all the peoples of Europe. Doesn't the richness of Europe consist precisely in its cultural diversity, in its various languages and mentalities? To constrain them under a unifying idea, a common cultural superstructure, could only lead to an obliteration of cultural diversity. As a European aspiration, that would be profoundly anti-European. And therein lies the deficit: that economic interests establish a unity where no unifying cultural commonality does or can exist. Haven't all attempts to subsume the economic project under some sort of cultural concept failed—and failed miserably? The Christian West? What about the Jews and the Muslims? The cradle of democracy? Take a look at the Greeks!

A common European culture: that's where the deficit would lie!

And the threatening arrogation: that the bureaucrats in Brussels, given their mania for regulations, might just come up with the idea of creating a European cultural policy!

Time and again the same criticism: the EU is just capital; it has nothing to do with culture.

And, time and again, the anticipatory criticism: woe to those in Brussels who now try to add cultural policy to the mix! That's just what we need, that the cultures in Europe, including maybe even artistic production and the art markets also become regulated by those bureaucrats in Brussels . . .

To some extent, both arguments are quite wrong and misunderstand reality. Creating a Europe that actively learns from its devastating history was, from the outset, a good idea. And that's exactly the unifying common idea that's always missing from considerations of the European project. You cannot separate the project's economic implications from its historical and philosophical ones, just as the idea itself refers to and directly arises from the intellectual history of Europe—that is, as a reaction to the murderous ideologies that reduced the continent to rubble. That idea, first and foremost, is a concrete utopia—a cultural, ideological and, if you will, superstructural phenomenon: a dictate of unmediated capitalist logic. That a utopia, if it is to materialize, can only have a chance if it takes root in the economic soil, that is, if it functions in the concrete production of real life, is arguably the only proposition that Marxists as well as Chicago boys, Keynesians as well as Hayekians, indeed, all professors—from philosophers to numismatists—can agree upon. And therein lay the brilliance of the idea: to extract the roots of nationalism by interlocking and interlinking the economies; to not only reconcile the hostile nations but, as a result of the national economies' interdependencies to completely transcend the nation-states, thereby creating genuine, permanent peace. And as everyone knows, everything we call culture and associate with it develops better in peacetime than in the deprivation and destruction of war and war economy.

As a project rooted in peace and freedom, the European Union is also essentially a cultural and political project. And the importance the economy plays in that project doesn't constitute the problem but, rather, its strength. The economy is the concrete basis according to which every idea must prove itself; it's the reality that, as the most recent decades have gradually shown, doesn't resist the idea but evolves it. And that also means—something many EU critics still can't imagine—that no agreement has yet been reached as to how, with what relations of production, the people on the continent ultimately would like to or will manage their economy. There is only one thing inherent to the idea of the EU and its implementation in reality: Europeans will increasingly have to manage their economy in solidarity.

The criticism that the EU is merely a capitalist project lacking a unifying idea is nonsense; the thesis that a unifying idea and a 'common culture' in Europe are completely impossible, an even greater nonsense; and the cheerfully ironic tootling that the EU mercifully doesn't even care about cultural policy, a scandal. For just when people criticize the EU due to the primacy of the economy, they need to demand a more aggressive, self-assertive and better-endowed cultural policy. The fact that that would be considered an arrogation (according to the essays of certain European intellectuals) constitutes yet another wacky example of how things that are being called into question on the European level are considered self-evident and, curiously enough, even being demanded at the national level. No one, for example, has ever seriously criticized the fact that national cultural policy in Germany or Austria destroys the country's cultural diversity or functions as a mere fig leaf for a highly problematic national economy. 'At home', it's clear to everyone that cultural policy is about creating parameters for promoting cultural and artistic life, and for promoting conditions conducive to cultural diversity. I cannot understand why such support is only considered legitimate and possible for nation-states. If anything, funding the diversity of European cultures and their exchange could productively open up national monocultures (I need only think of the German theatrical landscape!) and especially the unrealistic coupling of dominant national cultures.

In point of fact, European cultural policy has achieved—with embarrassingly modest means—long-term successes which cannot be valued highly enough. The Erasmus Programme, the Erasmus Mundus Programme, the Leonardo Programme and an array of other initiatives are brilliant achievements of a successful European cultural and educational policy at a time when national educational policy has become the vapid management of misery.

The problem, or even the arrogation, is not the demand that there has to be a European cultural policy but that the nation-states nowadays barely want to give it any assets.

The European Commission's cultural department is, in budgetary terms, the worst one. It is poorly financed and hardly taken seriously—even within the Commission itself. Accordingly, a commissioner nominated from France, Germany, the UK or Italy would never accept that assignment. Even Austria protested vigorously when a rumour briefly circulated that, to form the cabinet of Barroso II, the commissioner nominated by Austria could be assigned to culture. The largest newspaper in the 'cultural nation Austria' ran a headline in huge letters: 'THEY'RE FOBBING CULTURE OFF ON US!' A storm of indignation followed. That was funny—and also sad.

When the Austrian subsequently received a department with a big budget, the same newspaper rejoiced (to the tune of 'Once Again, We're a Force To Be Reckoned With!') and then went right back to its EU bashing.

Within the Commission, I was told how little prestige and importance the cultural department has among the commissioners. Whenever, for instance, the commissioner for competition or the commissioner for agriculture has to go to the bathroom during a Commission meeting, the meeting is suspended until the commissioner returns. When the commissioner for culture has to go to the bathroom, the other commissioners simply continue. How sad.

Only the smallest countries—Cyprus, for example (a tiny island or, in European terms, even less: half of a tiny island)—are assigned to culture. That's the reason why the career-conscious, top-ranking officials in that department primarily work on getting moved to another department; why only the doors in that directorate general are always closed, its personnel timidly hunkered down; and why the engaged civil servants in that department are typically—and appealingly, indeed, almost endearingly—depressed.

Whoever in Europe is not attending to rescuing banks, or has no need to court the votes of virtual illiterates in his or her nation-state, should criticize that state of affairs instead of ridiculing the idea of a European cultural policy, that is, the foundation of European politics.

23

In every respect, culture is the poorest department in the structure of the European Union. It hardly has a budget, hardly has responsibilities and hardly has any importance. Cultural policy could remain the domain of the individual member states. Up until now, the cultural commissioner has never been prominent, even to the most attentive European observer. What should that person say anyway? What should that commissioner comment upon? Everything that's talked about nowadays, everything of interest to the European public sphere, is beyond his or her responsibilities—if not formally, then at least factually. The crisis is not that person's responsibility, and what his or her responsibility is is unclear, unclear to that person, at any rate.

I wanted to understand things better. What kind of people work in that department? What do they do? What does their day-to-day look like? Do they have to be able to do more than just write nice homilies? Is there a sense of, a concept for or, at a minimum, a discussion about what European cultural policy could be?

You would think that, in these times, with the Commission's Berlaymont building humming like a beehive owing to the financial crisis, one department might still remain quiet and calm, untouched by the flurry of activity: culture—where sensitive, sophisticated people patiently work at facilitating and mediating European culture and its diverse richness, against which even American rating agencies can't compete.

But as a matter of fact, the one department where, for a long time, it seemed impossible to set up an appointment for a conversation and get some information that would go beyond what I could download on my computer at home was the culture department. Then, through a pincer movement of interventions by the Austrian ambassador to the EU and Barroso's office, I was finally able to get an appointment—with Deputy Chief of Cabinet Themis Christophidou. Even in the preliminary stages, as we were setting up the appointment, she appeared slightly indignant because I was trying to force my way into her fully booked calendar. Forty minutes, she emailed me, would be the absolute maximum. There was no way she had any more time than that. I wrote back to her that that would surely be enough time, providing she spoke quickly.

I received no further written response from her—and she met me for a meeting at which I was thrown out of her conference room after just a few minutes. The following conversation took place:

THEMIS CHRISTOPHIDOU. I've been told you're writing a book.

ROBERT MENASSE. Yes, that's correct.

TC. I don't understand why you want to speak to me. My spokesman can give you all the statistical information you need.

RM. I don't need any statistical information. I'm writing a novel.

TC. A novel? Why, for heaven's sake, are you writing a novel?

RM. I'm a novelist.

TC. What does that have to do with me?

RM. Nothing, or, rather, only indirectly. I'm writing a novel in which one of the characters is an official with the Commission. That's why I'm interested in—

TC. Does that person know you're writing a novel about him or her? Did that person give you permission? What kind of book is it supposed to be? A biography?

RM. You misunderstood me. I said it's a novel. Fiction. Understand?

TC. If you're writing fiction, then why do you need documents from us?

RM. I didn't say I needed documents. In order to be able to write my novel, I'd like to have a sense of what it is people here do. What the everyday work is like. How the whole thing runs. I thought perhaps you could tell me—

TC. Listen, I don't have the slightest interest in talking about my work. And I'm even less interested in becoming a character in a novel. (*She stands up and walks to the door.*) A novel! Fiction! That's crazy, you know!

RM (*standing up and walking to the door*). Sorry to have wasted your time.

TC (*opening the door*). It's my job.

RM. That wasting time is your job was information about your work!

TC says *adieu* and I'm out of the door.

On the evening of that same day, I met by chance the European commissioner for competition at a reading by a Greek novelist in the bookstore Passa Porta in Sainte Catherine.

'Here in Brussels so much is going on culturally,' he said. 'And I especially love the events at Passa Porta. They bring great writers from all over the world here!'

I asked him if he ever meets his colleague, the commissioner for culture, at those readings on occasion.

He looked at me, smiled and said, 'No, I've never seen her at a reading, or at the opera or an art opening. Culture isn't a question of one's department, you know!' He laughed. 'Here in Brussels I'd say: *au contraire!*' He laughed heartily. 'By the way,' he said, 'do you see the man over there with the five-o'clock shadow? He's the commissioner for regional policy!'

24

Subsequent to its bold beginning and its series of fascinating advances, such is the current dissatisfying, problematic and critical state of European development. The Treaty of Lisbon dramatically weakened the Commission, even though the Commission is supposed to be the very institution propelling the integration of member states and incrementally implementing the standardization of parameters. In the medium to long term, the Commission is also supposed to develop into the actual government of a conjoined Europe but, instead, it has been cut back to a glorified secretary's office for the nation-states, especially for the conservative heads of government and for the German chancellor. Within the Commission, culture and education is the weakest department—a largely powerless one—because in those areas the nation-states are unwilling to cede sovereignty and allocate funds, even though the EU, as a peace project, is essentially also a great cultural-political project. That doesn't mean, however, that you can extrapolate that the European project is purely an economic one, a union promoted and held together by capitalist and economic interests since, for the longest time, the European Council has blocked a joint economic policy.

To be sure, the Treaty of Lisbon also strengthened the Parliament, but it still has not been endowed with full parliamentary rights. Moreover, due to voting rights, the Parliament must struggle internally—and not necessarily productively—with the contradiction between supranationality and nationalism. It can't even be said that the nation-states have refused to accept a rational European electoral law, as they have yet to entertain a discussion about it. In elections for the European Parliament, voters can only cast national ballots. Given the state of things, that's grotesque enough. National parties send members to the European Parliament, who are then denied full parliamentary rights by the Council of nation-states. It can, of course, happen that a candidate from a national ballot becomes an active member of the European Parliament. There are countless examples of that. Although fortuitous, the system is not set up that way. As far as I'm concerned, European democracy should not be a matter of luck. Do you know how many candidates the national parties nominate to ballots for European elections so that they can be disposed of in Brussels because they have become domestic political liabilities and the party doesn't know what else to do with them? I don't think the European Parliament should turn into a political waste-management facility. Do you know how many members of the European Parliament are elected from populist anti-EU parties? The election law regulating national ballots literally facilitates that large numbers of nationalistic anti-Europeans get elected to the European Parliament from their respective nation-states, thus frequently forcing unproductive disputes between European parliamentarians and those who simply want to obstruct parliament. As far as I'm concerned, the European Parliament shouldn't become the central meeting point for anti-Europeans.

At any rate, it's no wonder so many voters have no interest in the Parliament. The Parliament's modest upgrade in the Treaty of Lisbon came at much too high a price. It was paid for by the massive upgrade to and strengthening of the European Council. The Council received its own permanent president, which constitutes a brilliant act of European self-sabotage. Now the Council has two presidents, so to speak: the rotating president of the current presidency country and the perma-nent president. In addition, there's the president of the Commission, who previously was considered to be the 'EU president' but subsequently has been deported to a kind of parallel universe. And then there is the president of the European Parliament, whose communication with the Commission—which has the power to propose legislation and is thus a natural ally of the Parliament—gets squelched by the Council's millstones. It's an unreasonable construct, the intent of which was to serve a supranational system that is covered—indeed, disfigured—by the birthmarks of old nationalism. It's not just the only political system with four presidents wrangling over power. Most notably, it's the only political system in the history of political systems in which the institution endowed with the greatest power repeatedly opposes the establishing intent of the system and refuses to accept the political objectives delineated in the community treaty. That institution, of course, is the Council.

Engagement for a democratic Europe, the conflict over the Union's so clearly avowed—yet so indistinctly defined—democratic deficit and the 'citizens' rage' should all be directed against the Council. As the preconditions for a democratic Europe, a democratic offensive should demand: abolishing the Council, endowing the Parliament with full parliamentary rights and no longer electing the members of Parliament through national elections but, rather, regional ones. Isn't that what we were promised—a postnational, subsidiary and regional Europe?

As someone who lives in Vienna, I, for example, am much closer geographically and also in terms of mentality to Bratislava, Slovakia or Sopron, Hungary than to Bludenz or even Klagenfurt in Austria. What national-patriotic interests am I supposed to share with people in Bludenz or Klagenfurt? If I do have common interests with people in Bludenz, then that has nothing to do with Austria; it's because people in Vienna—just like people in Bludenz or in Darmstadt or in Bolzano or in Coimbra or somewhere else—have an interest in reasonable parameters within which everyone can try to live their lives with dignity and decency. Why should the parameters only 55 kilometres east of where I live be different just because a national border happens to be located there while 650 kilometres to the west—a place I rarely go to—I can count on the same national parameters? Fifteen kilometres farther, however, they're different again.

Under common parameters, citizens in their particular places of residency and within their particular regions can live their collective lives according to their respective cultures and mentalities, according to their respective traditions and innovative capabilities, and according to their respective local requirements and needs—that is, they can imbue the subsidiarity* established in the European constitution with democratic life. Essentially, that's precisely the development the European Union has long since initiated: standardizing social parameters together with social differentiation through subsidiarity. What significance, what rationale does an intermediary entity such as the 'nation-state' still have? It can no longer be rationally justified. One potential response could be that not everything in life has to be rationally justified and it is, after all, possible to be happy even in irrational circumstances. In social and political activity, however, there are no examples of how irrational conditions could have promoted the greatest possible happiness of the majority. On the contrary. Whoever doesn't see that or thinks it's unimportant abandons the greatest accomplishment of European history and, at the same time, the substance of Europe's future, namely, a commitment to the Enlightenment.

25

Following a discussion about 'The Crisis and the Future of Europe' at the Deutsches Theater in Berlin, the organizers invited the panelists to dinner. At the table, I sat down next to a journalist, a long-time correspondent in Brussels, who said to me: You said a lot of very interesting and important things, but your idea about the nations necessarily dying off is completely crazy!

Why? I asked.

I think having a national identity is important. It's nice. I'd miss it if I didn't have one.

What, for example, would you miss?

I don't know. Belonging. Identity, that is. I'm a German, you know. Not French or Spanish or something else. That defines me. Why should that no longer be important?

What does that mean concretely? Give me an example, please. What is typically German and has shaped you so much that you can say: that's part of my being, my approach to life, my sense of self and, at the same time, connects me to all the other Germans, and that makes me happy, and that's why I'm a German and proud of having that nationality? Give me one single example. But please don't say the beautiful landscape. I find that response preposterous in Austria. Besides, a landscape is never national. At most, the only thing national about a landscape is a particular way of aestheticizing or ideologically charging it. And please don't say the language. There are German speakers in other nations. And please don't say the legal situation or the German Constitution. Couldn't you imagine a European constitutional patriotism? And please don't say German culture. As someone from the Rhineland, you weren't at all shaped by Bavarian or Hanseatic culture. You were shaped by regional culture and then by your interest in the cultural diversity of the world. So give me an example. What's typically German and provides you with an appealing national identity?

I don't know. All kinds of things. For example . . . She raised her hands and said exasperatedly: There are so many things. Little things, perhaps, but they're important! German bread, for instance.

Just then, the waiter set a bread basket on the table. She looked at it, and I thought: that *German* bread is called a *baguette*!

26

Democratically revolutionizing Europe: the regions—which, as everyone knows, in most cases do not stop at national borders (which have already disappeared anyway)—elect their representatives to Parliament. Parliament elects the commissioners and the Commission's president. The Commission, the only truly European institution, develops the bills and guidelines, which Parliament then votes on.

That's how the major parameters can be defined: the financial, economic and tax policies together with the legal and social systems. And whatever can be regionally decided remains with the regional parliaments. All that would be comprehensible, could be voted upon (and instituted or not, depending on the outcome of the vote), would strengthen every individual's consciousness as a European and would also be consistent with peoples' intrinsic self-understanding, their true identity. People are actually rooted in their region, shaped by life in their region. What is 'national identity' compared to a sense of home? Having a home is a human right, having a national identity is not. Home is where scents and cadences strike a particular chord, the concrete place in life where one isn't a visitor, where linguistic peculiarities and idiosyncratic traditions don't necessarily imply affirmation but surely a sense of affiliation. Home is the only place where what's diffuse and obscure becomes clear and concrete, where the bread tastes especially good, where emotions are greater and the anger over small-mindedness is as great as the love of expansive thought. A regional identity is the root of a European one.

Nationalism is dying off. In the medium term, national parliaments can also be abolished. In that kind of Europe, we would no longer have to contend with such irrational phenomenon as David Cameron—even though his country doesn't even participate in the European Monetary Union—being able to block a common European fiscal policy so that he can protect his financial speculation market: the City of London. Then he could attend with greater concentration to the question of why, thanks to his national politics, half of England is on fire. That would be much better for everyone.

27

For those to whom it sounds too utopian: a year before they were signed, the Treaties of Rome seemed totally unrealistic. The fall of the Wall was utterly utopian the day before it happened. If there's one historical experience belonging to my generation, then it's this: the so-called pragmatic reasoning of the so-called realists is nothing but history's laughing stock. On account of our experiences, it's my generation's responsibility to call out, over and over again, to the political elites: 'Think about the Treaties of Rome and remember the fall of the Berlin

Wall! Much more is possible than what you think is doable today!'

28

European political pragmatists and many critics of the European project have more in common than they think they do. They're linked by their blindness about the future and the inability to recognize the dynamics within the status quo that coercively extend beyond it. It should be politics' business to turn those dynamics into a propulsive force for structural changes, the goals of which need to be communicated to society. But, instead, the status quo is administered, and the symptoms of its internal contradictions along with the consequences of its internal dynamics are discussed at crisis summits. Decisions are no longer made with a goal worth reaching in mind but, rather, with a view towards managing the status quo's crisis. 'Deficit' is understood as the budget deficit of a member state, and not as the objective, actual deficit—that is, the difference between the ideals and reality of the European idea. Desirable, first and foremost, would be a common policy for at least the community of the Monetary Union, but politics thinks only about yesterday and wants to make sure that the individual nation-states, each on its own—in the future as in the past—doesn't stand out on account of its national budget.

And the criticism: it also grapples with the deficits—but it, too, doesn't grapple with the objective deficits the collective project still has in terms of its idea and its aspirations. It doesn't see what remains unfulfilled. It doesn't recognize in the dynamics of the situation what's desirable and needs to be achieved. It doesn't attach itself to what has been lost. For the critics as well, the status quo is a crisis scenario, and they want to save the status quo from the future instead of redeeming it in the future. Just like the politics they criticize, they also think only about yesterday. Looking backward, they are shocked by the differences the European project already has compared to the respective national systems (for instance, in terms of democracy or in terms of the nation-states' previous sovereign possibilities regarding currency and economic policies) instead of seeing that the European project must transcend them for good historical reasons. The criticism of the EU critics is, unfortunately, too often reminiscent of the criticism of those early scholars who complained that with the invention of printing the beauty of handwriting will be lost.

29

The heads of state in the European Council defend national interests and the final remains of national sovereignty; critics of the EU defend their national democracies and want to strengthen them vis-à-vis the juggernaut that is 'Brussels'. Both feel validated in their engagement and propelled by the crisis, which, as we repeatedly are told, really threatens vested interests, destroys what has already been attained, exacts victims and effectively cannot be overcome by democratic means within the given structures. The crisis seems to prove that the

European project is too large and cannot work—that is to say, the price to rescue it is too high. Initially, it was paid for with sovereignty rights; now—and in the unforeseeable future—with national wealth. Initially, democracy was damaged; now, austerity is strangulating the social-welfare state—the best thing, that is, that post-fascist democracies in Europe established and the indispensable prerequisite for a stable democracy.

Those who defend or sugarcoat the national, who, for the first time in almost a century have resumed their place in the centre of society, don't realize what, in fact, they're doing. They are the ones manufacturing the crisis, and the more they defend themselves against it using their means, the more they exacerbate it.

The current crisis is precisely the result of resisting the logical and systematic progression of postnational Europe. The postnational development, the linkage of European states and their interdependencies have progressed to such an extent that national solutions to problems—economic or otherwise—are no longer possible. At the same time, renationalization has increased so much—not only as a disposition but also politically and institutionally—through the strengthening of the Council within the European system, so that systematic supranational solutions are no longer possible either. Since collective solutions to the crisis, however, would definitely be possible—not to mention the fact that the current crisis would never even have escalated to the extent it has had it not been for the constant harassment from the defenders of national interests—it is very clear where the problem at present lies: the culprits, of all people, are now posing as the saviours, having interpreted the effects of their decisions as the cause of their next decisions.

As a matter of fact, the crisis never was a financial crisis, and it never will be—even if it were to cost 10 times as much— a financial crisis in the true sense of the term. It lacks all the defining characteristics of a financial crisis. A sum in the amount of 2 per cent of Europe's GNP does not justify being called a 'financial crisis'. Securities trading and speculating on the stock market are functioning without the slightest indication of an impending market crash. Following the rectified bubbles in the market for new technologies and the real estate market, there is nothing that looks even remotely like a bubble (other than the politicians' speech bubbles). Money is not lacking (the money supply is a political decision); assets back all the debts (whether the assets are taxed and the resulting proceeds are then invested in the indebted societies or whether the debts and assets are reduced by a haircut is a political decision). No bank threatens to collapse. On the contrary, capital is being virtually forced upon the banks, and if a bank were to collapse, the deposits would be insured. Greece's budget deficits do not justify talk of a 'European financial crisis', nor do they justify Germany's financial policy of behaving like Europe's schoolmaster. In 2011, Germany had the highest tax revenue and hence the highest budget in its history since the founding of the state—but it still didn't have a balanced budget. Currently, Germany has debts of 579.9 billion euros above the allowable rate of 60 per cent of the GDP. If, given the current German economic situation and the exemplary German tax discipline, no budget is possible without increasing indebtedness, what does that tell us?

The crisis is, of course, a political crisis, but it is not the political crisis of a single EU member state or of a few member states. It is the political crisis of the Union as a whole. It arose and assumed its magnitude due to the deadlocked discrepancies within the EU's political-institutional system. And it can only be solved through a systematic further development of that political system, through correcting its internal contradictions. The crisis is the indisputable result of the by now completely obsolete compromises institutionalized in the Union's political constitution. The EU is a bold project to transcend nationalism and the nation-states on the continent. It necessarily arose from historical experiences and has been legitimized by its own history as the longest period of European peace. At the beginning, representatives of the nation-states had to assemble. Given the current state of affairs, however, it is no longer justifiable to have—in-between the two supranational European institutions, the Parliament and the Commission—a third institution, the European Council, that stands in systematic contradiction to postnational development and whose power and authority, moreover, contrary to the rationality of that postnational development, was recently strengthened.

We can see where weakening the Commission, restricting the rights of the Parliament and strengthening the Council— that reverse thrust of history, that EU Thermidor—leads, but we see it under an incorrect name: the financial crisis.

Political engagement, democratic struggle and cosmopolitan energy must now be rationally directed at abolishing the Council. The Council must be done away with! And not replaced. In-between a European Parliament that elects a government (the commissioners) that has the European Commission at its disposal, there is no logical and necessary place for an institution such as the European Council.

That's why I'm such a great fan of the crisis. I'm keen on the crisis. Fear not! The crisis will greatly and, most likely, decisively advance Europe. I don't say that because I derive childish optimism from the stale phrase 'Every crisis is an opportunity.' That phrase, of course, is nonsense. The opportunities existed earlier but since they weren't properly made use of, the crisis developed. The crisis isn't an opportunity; the crisis is coercion. At the risk of an otherwise impending demise of Europe, the crisis will exact those political solutions and the reform of the European constitution that, owing to nation-state small-mindedness, had not been previously possible.

30

The evidence is growing. The political elites, the heads of government and the foreign ministers of the member states are beginning to hide their remorse on account of their previous failures behind new, bold phrases. 'Deepening the political union', 'Ceding more sovereignty to Brussels', 'United States of Europe' and the like. Their empty phrases are only bold compared to the statements they made yesterday, but they're not bold considering the real requirements of the Union and its desirable development. What would be necessary now is by no means a discussion along the lines of 'We're really in hot water now, let's try something unimaginative but somehow different!' What's needed is a discussion to clarify crucial questions: What should European democracy look like? How can it take shape and be cast in a constitution?

I'm not interested in what politicians—whom I couldn't elect and whom I don't even want to legitimize through tolerating, but who lay claim to 'leadership' in Europe—now force through as new regulations to solve the crisis they themselves caused based on the given constitution, even if they, which is complicated enough, have to stretch and change the treaties a little here and there. I'm interested in the question: How will that which has never been, that which is historically completely new, that internationally innovative, bold, European avantgarde project, look—the project of postnational democracy?

At the Bureau of European Policy Advisors, the think tank of the European Commission, people are thinking about that. Here and there, stimulating and worthwhile research and position papers by philosophers (for example, Jürgen Habermas, Oskar Negt) are being published addressing the question. But the discussion does not permeate public discourse; the fascinating aspects of the question do not galvanize public minds despite their excitability—not to mention the masses who call for more plebiscitary democracy, but by that mean wanting to institute the death penalty in their country instead of discussing the question of how postnational democracy would have to be organized, a question they think probably only a fool would pose.

And yet, that question is decisive for the future of Europe. Its widespread discussion is essential for creating the necessary political pressure that will lead to reforming the European constitution, advancing the European project and, finally, fulfilling the promise that, at the outset of the journey, was so strong it enabled the journey to be undertaken in the first place.

The problem thus lies clearly before us: what we understand as 'democracy' is a means of political organization that, for the optimal participation of its citizens and the representation of their interests, was developed in and for nation-states. 'Democracy', in the form we know it by, is a product of the nineteenth century. It is inextricably bound to nation-building, just as, conversely, nation-building was engaged in by the heroes of democratic movements. The model's roots lie in the French Revolution, whose emphasis on freedom, equality and brotherhood led, through an intricate dialectic, to the idea and invention of the nation. In Germany and, subsequently, in Austria and other European countries, the idea was adopted but without being able to invoke a successful revolution. Wars, yes. Civil wars, yes. And then, somehow, a nation and democracy. But that nineteenth-century product was hapless. Constitutional monarchies were swept away or turned into operetta productions; democratic republics flashed briefly like a bolt of lightning. And then it was dark.

Given the enmity among nations, both the nations and their democracies proved defenceless and, when nineteenth century ended in the middle of the twentieth, the continent was a pile of rubble. Then came a new beginning, which no one fought for, and no one really considered a victory, not only in the German-speaking countries but—according to how generously you interpret things—also in 20 or 24 of the current member states of the European Union. What we have practised in our lifetime as democracy, what we have understood as democracy, the little we have learnt about the term 'democracy' had been given to us and—as much more than the Austrian example shows—was immediately put into nation-building. When the Stalinist states imploded, we—at the end of the twentieth century—had to once again experience from front-row seats: Yugoslavia first had to be shattered by nationalistic civil wars because nations first had to emerge from the territory of that state in order to then convert the authoritarian structures into democratic ones. The slivers of the destroyed states, now nation-states, will, one by one, be admitted to the EU. Why couldn't they just admit Yugoslavia? Because they didn't know any better. There had to be untold suffering because no other kind of democracy was familiar to them except for nation-state democracy. Thus nation-states first had to be bombed; democratic structures are a condition for being accepted into the EU. That seemed so logical to everyone that no one noticed the contradiction: that the same European politicians who pursued the expansion of Germany, its so-called reunification, were simultaneously involved in the disintegration of Yugoslavia as a precondition for its EU suitability. They didn't consider it a contradiction because, for them, both cases were about the same thing: becoming a nation. That, of course, is completely grotesque if you recall that, in the case of the European project, it was and is a question of transcending nationalism. At the same time, of course, it's also—and essentially—a question of a democratic Europe, which takes us right back to the centre of the problem, the solution to which will decide Europe's future. Our democracy, our conceptions of democracy, our experiences with democracy, our expectations for democracy, everything, that is, that we consider to be desirable democratic standards—all that always was and is national democracy. It was an intelligent, bold and, subsequent to all the historical experiences, the only correct idea to build a Europe that transcends nationalism. Of course, that prospective postnational Europe should be a democratic Europe, but suddenly those two basic requirements for the continent's peaceful future—both of which are so logically interrelated and so logically derived from history—appear to be contradictory. National democracy obstructs postnational development; postnational development destroys democracy.

Is the contradiction irreconcilable? If so, then it would be necessary to decide against Europe . . . and in favour of nationalistic conflicts with all their consequences, which are perpetually possible because they've existed throughout history.

The contradiction, of course, can be resolved—but, as a first step, it's necessary to become aware of the contradiction and then decide that in the twenty-first century we should finally put an end to the nineteenth century. Then, for the time being, it's necessary to warm up to the idea of forgetting about democracy and abolishing its institutions insofar as they are national institutions—that is, seeing to the demise of that model of democracy that appears so sacred and valuable to us because it's familiar to us. We need to push what's going to fall anyway when the European project succeeds. We need to break the final taboo of enlightened societies: that our democracy is a sacred good.

And we need to devise a new form of democracy, one that is not coupled with the idea of the nation-state. It's imperative to be clear about this. Postnational democracy cannot have the same form, the same internal structure that national democracies developed. You simply cannot hoist elements of national democracies piecemeal onto a supranational level and combine them. In that kind of sublation, too much gets left behind—and what doesn't get left behind at that higher level can no longer be reached from the bottom. The ultimate result can only be a vast superstate which then either turns into a supernation or gets ripped to pieces trying to become one. As a matter of fact, previous attempts to raise portions of national democracies to a supranational level, thereby giving them a glint of democratic legitimacy, have ultimately led only to unproductive contradictions—for instance, what we currently call the crisis.

The question of how postnational European democracy—in contrast to the national democracies of Europe—could look is repeatedly suppressed by the ostensibly urgent and seemingly pragmatic discussion about how the legal capacity of schizophrenic political elites (who are the national heads of state and simultaneously members of a comprehensive European decision-making body, the European Council) could be guaranteed. The crisis produces, in turn, the pressure to somehow break through the aporia and change the rules of the game, but it's still the case that ignorance is thrilled to be replaced by a lack of imagination. The same politicians who—up until yesterday, if not to say, early this morning—considered it their primary tasks to defend national interests and project an image to their constituents as combatants against the unreasonable demands that 'Brussels' (which, of course, is they themselves) seeks to impose upon their nation suddenly realized by noon, at five to twelve, that the problems they had produced by doing so could not be solved by the means at hand. They therefore started dreaming about a 'political deepening of the Union', ceding more sovereignty to 'Brussels', and more centralized, collective competence. And what does their lack of imagination dream up, what is the image that appears before their eyes: that the European Union must continue to develop into a 'United States of Europe modelled on the USA!' The foreign ministers of the European member states debated and dreamt. Then, in June 2012, they appeared before the press and said: This is our present point of view, United States of Europe modelled on the USA.

Such a statement allows us to see once again with deplorable clarity that this generation of politicians is a lost one, a transitional generation. It can no longer comprehend what was at stake when the European project began, and it cannot yet comprehend where the project's dynamics should lead. And it is precisely this no-longer-not-yet that is Europe's crisis. The European project was never planned or conceived of as an incremental approximation of the United States of America. You can't infer that even from Winston Churchill's famous speech in Zurich in September 1946 in which he initially formulated the expression 'United States of Europe' as an epochal idea. He literally spoke of '*a kind* of United States', and in the context of his speech it becomes obvious that he clearly had a new, a completely different kind in mind. The formulation was a metaphor, essentially conveying the following message: the age-old animosities among the European nations must finally be overcome. Furthermore, Churchill alluded to the Continent in his speech, excluding—as he clearly stated—the UK's participation. But a European superstate modelled on the USA and across from the UK, on the other side of the Channel, was surely the last thing he was imagining.

A European US, of course, is utter nonsense, an absolute perversion of the basic concept of the European project. Europe will be something totally new; the USA is the old European project, which developed conventionally according to the mechanisms we are currently transcending in Europe. Why is the USA an old European project? The USA is the product of immigrants who brought their ideas and methods from Europe, proceeding accordingly—violent conquests of territory, wars of unification and nation-building. That is the complete opposite of what Europe stands for today: expansion through negotiations and agreeing on common values, unification as a peace project and dissolution of the nation-states through a postnational community.

During the past 60 years—in which the European peace project grew—the USA waged approximately 35 wars, intervened with armed forces, engaged in military invasions without United Nations resolutions and initiated or supported putsches and coups. In dozens of countries, they've installed military and so-called security advisors. The USA has never explained what young men from Texas or Ohio were doing armed with weapons in the Bay of Pigs* or Grenada.* They've never explained why the USA had to overthrow the elected president of a sovereign nation and replace him with a fascist dictator—as, for example, they did in Chile. But then, they didn't need to explain that because it was clear to all the old Europeans: that's how you defend national interests. The Monroe Doctrine, constitutive of the constitution of the US nation, is a law that would not be possible in today's Europe: declaring every military invasion, every murder legitimate if they serve to defend national interests.

A Europe that becomes a supernation, a centralized superstate 'defending' its 'interests' with armed forces in the Hindu Kush or in a war over the oil fields in Sudan was never the Europe the founding fathers of the European project had in mind—and it cannot and must not become the Europe we acknowledge as our lesson from the bloody history of this continent and as our mandate.

It's important to dream a lot. It's important to discuss and debate a lot. Ultimately, something completely new will emerge. Not a supernation but a continent without nations, a free association of regions. No superstatist centralism but lived democratic subsidiarity with a centre in which truly communal institutions develop sensible parameters and safeguard legal certainty. Is it worth fighting for? What is engaging in defending the democracy that was given to us compared to that?

31

Whoever cannot imagine all this should at least try to imagine what Auschwitz means. What it means for us up until now as well as in perpetuity. And why, since the founding of the European Commission, every president of the Commission has commenced his term in office with a trip to Auschwitz.

Now the nationalists will derisively holler: 'There he goes again with the fascism cudgel!'

Fascism is the cudgel, not the memory of it.

32

'Cheque, please!'

Sure, we can check the numbers.

In 1953, a German delegation crawled on its knees to London to beg for debt relief at an international conference.* The burden of debt arising from the reparations they were expected to pay for two world wars was crushing Germany. In response to Greece's initiative, Germany's 22 creditor nations—whose cities' infrastructures were destroyed by the delusions of German nationalism and whose populations were in part systematically exterminated (for example, half the inhabitants of Thessaloniki in Greece)—those states, at Greece's request, resolved to grant the Germans a debt reduction. The postwar German 'economic miracle' could not have happened without that debt relief.

Prior to the London Debt Agreement, Germany had a debt ratio of 21 per cent of its GDP. After the agreement was implemented in 1958, Germany could reduce its debt ratio to just 6 per cent.

Greece's current sevenfold debt ratio makes Germany—which took to begging due to what it considered its once staggeringly crushing debts—react mercilessly. At the same time, the German debt ratio has by now increased from 6 to approximately 80 per cent.

Germany promised to pay its remaining debts, which were radically reduced following the London Agreement, in gradual instalments. In 1990, Germany discontinued its payments to—of all countries—Greece. There might be plenty of reasons for that: reunification was very expensive and it was necessary to economize somewhere else; a Greek minister would rather pocket 1 million himself than see 25 million go into the budget. (I'm referring here to the German press, which, as well informed as it is, claimed that the Greeks are 'corrupt'.) In compliance with the German press law, though, I don't want to allege anything and so decisively dismiss that conjecture. At any rate, according to the radical debt reduction of the London Agreement of 1953, it's a fact that Germany still has 3.5 billion euros in outstanding debts to Greece. And that doesn't include the interest.

In a 1990 dispatch, Germany announced the 'imminent payment of the outstanding balance'—but has yet to do so.

'We haven't asked for the cheque!'

33

Who wants that democracy? That ratcheting up of national emotions for which only those whose national rage was fomented have to pay?

34

I don't know what a completely new postnational democracy will look like. I only know we must discuss the issue, with increasing knowledge of what it entails. It's not about forming a superstate. The fantasies about the importance of Europe conducting global politics in the future 'on a par with the superpowers' are nonsense. No normal person has a basic need to be a taxpayer to a superpower, and if somebody does need that, then that person should receive psychotherapy in a sensible social system.

It's also not about centralism. Subsidiarity was what we were promised, and it's no contradiction to that promise to have our collective institutions located in one city. It's also not about sublating the nations in a great supranation. That, of course, would be pure folly. It's about creating a constitution for a free and peaceful Europe of regions.

For the first time, there's a revolutionary subject that can not only triumph but also redeem what the idea of a revolutionary subject promised us: the liberation of everyone through the liberation of a universal class. Never before has an oppressed class seized power through resistance, uprisings and revolutions, not to mention establishing universal liberation, peace, justice and a truly civil society. Slaves in slaveholding societies rose up; the slaveholding societies perished; however, the new ruling class did not consist of the former slaves but the feudal lords. The indentured servants they oppressed revolted; peasant wars occurred; the feudal system perished, but the new ruling class was not composed of those who fought against the old system, the peasants, but a new class that had arisen in the meantime, the bourgeoisie. The new antagonistic class, the proletariat, organized itself, rebelled and attempted revolutions. It was never a revolutionary class; it just wanted its share of social prosperity and recognition, but it was defeated and punished as if it had been a revolutionary class. Even where it seemingly did succeed, it didn't become the ruling class; a completely new class, which had arisen in the meantime, assumed power, the nomenklatura. Whoever fought them and thus contributed to the demise of that system had to then look on helplessly as a completely different group assumed power: populist nationalists, adventurers and carpetbaggers—or, in the case of the GDR, the party leaders of the neighbouring state.

For the first time in Europe, a truly universal class is emerging whose engagement will lead to a system of sustainable, universal law and freedom. The class is universal because, for the first time in history, it doesn't define itself sociologically as a class that, as a result of antagonistic contradictions, defines itself as the 'ruling class' while a new class emerges and seizes everything for itself. Instead, it is made up of all of Europe's classes, strata and groups that, given their highly diverse experiences and knowledge, bring their expertise to a movement criticizing national systems, criticizing aporias in the structure of the European Union and criticizing a form of globalization that is clearly not the globalization of human rights but of financial capital. Much of that is still uncomprehended, but a dynamic is arising, creating political pressure and increasing awareness in equal measure, which the system will ultimately not be able to contain.

35

Am I contradicting myself? I'm just contemplating.

Am I becoming downright euphoric? If so, my anxieties and fears will balance everything out.

36

Meanwhile, my German friend's post—'The EU will be our demise'—has been 'liked' hundreds of times; at the same time, it's long since disappeared from the realm of public awareness. That's how it is. That's the demise. What he simply calls 'our'—without any further specification, yet assuming general agreement—sinks peacefully and painlessly in the world of social media. To whom does that 'our' in that sentence so casually heralding 'our demise' refer? Surely not 'us Facebookers'. It more likely refers to 'us Germans'. Isn't it odd that it's communicated in a medium interconnecting friends in—I don't know how many—other countries? Or does he mean with that 'our' what he, in his self-understanding and that of his friends, considers to be the 'critical intelligentsia'? That, by the way, would be interesting. Then the sentence would have a dialectical meaning. We'll perish with everything we've learnt because we have to learn everything anew. In that case, the demise—according to the expectations of a critical intelligentsia—would be a salvation.

Either the Europe of nation-states will perish or the project to transcend those nation-states will. Either way, the EU will be 'our' demise. There isn't a third possibility. Either way, things will fall into place. Either Europe will once again—but this time peacefully—be the world's avant-garde or Europe will definitively prove to the world that abiding lessons cannot be learnt from history and that there is no humane way to turn beautiful utopias into a reality safeguarded by law. And if, in the latter case, the political doomsdayers are standing yet again in front of smouldering ruins, stammering affectedly—'This should never be allowed to happen again!'—then derisive laughter will roar from history's long, dark corridors.

37

At some point, I realized all the novels I've loved the most, the ones I've most ardently admired and those that have made the deepest impression on me—as different as they are in terms of subject matter, the times in which they were written and narrated time—can all be subsumed under one concept: they're all 'evening-before' novels. They all represent, as it were, the eve of an epochal rupture. Heimito von Doderer's *The Demons* (1956), Fyodor Dostoevsky's *Demons* (1872), Thomas Mann's

The Magic Mountain (1924) , Robert Musil's *The Man without Qualities* (1930–43), Joseph Roth's *Radetzky March* (1932), Theodor Fontane's *The Stechlin* (1898) and Guillermo Cabrera Infante's *Three Trapped Tigers* (1967), to name just a few.

Ever since, I've been preoccupied by the idea of writing a novel depicting the panorama of an epoch in which the characters, just like at any other time, have their worries, hopes, aspirations and problems, try to somehow manage them and fail, or somehow manage to neurotically sedate themselves, thereby maintaining a world they don't know about and can't even imagine it will no longer exist the next day. That's something our grandparents experienced first-hand. It's an experience we could observe in Europe starting in 1989, and almost certainly an experience we can have in the foreseeable future once it's decided whether the system of nation-states or the system transcending those nation-states perishes. Either way, we're living on the eve of demise. Our current situation resembles that of the characters in those great 'evening-before' novels—and in the spirit of those great novels, you, the reader, are now the 'hero'.

POSTSCRIPT

Since its publication in late summer 2012, this book has occasioned numerous panel discussions and interviews in almost every European country. I gladly participated in those discussions and interviews, in the course of which certain questions frequently arose. What follows is my attempt to summarize and respond to them.

Are you familiar with the following fable? A small bird, perhaps a sparrow—as you know, they're the ones who like to sing from the rooftops—lay on his back in a meadow, stretching his little legs in the air. There were threateningly low, dark clouds, and a strong wind was blowing. A stray tomcat appeared, came increasingly closer and wondered why the bird didn't fly away. He asked, 'Why are you, bird—a creature of the sky—lying so quiet on the ground, stretching your little legs in the air?'

The bird replied, 'You're attending to your business, so maybe you don't realize the sky is threatening to fall down'.

The cat was amused by the bird's imagination, but couldn't take him seriously, of course. 'And you think that by lifting your little feet in the air you can hold the sky up?'

'That, of course, is questionable,' the bird said. 'But isn't everything questionable? And I do have to do something, you know.'

'What would we do if we didn't have you?' the cat said sarcastically.

Did he eat the bird? Or did he spare him, aware of the fact that every biotope needs some dreamers? They do no harm, provide some amusement and later on you might even be able to incorporate their stories into some homilies. At any rate, the cat then quickly sought shelter. As I said, the dark clouds were threateningly low. First, he found a fox's den. That didn't lead to anything good. Then he found a comfortable hole in the ground, but that territory belonged to the skunks. He was thus forced to overcome his hydrophobia. But we're really not interested in the cat any more. Our interest belongs to the dreamers. And, occasionally, the dark clouds.

In what year was the following said: 'The day will come when you, France, you, Italy, you, England, and you, Germany—all the continent's peoples—will coalesce into a greater unity without having to lose your distinct features and your glorious uniqueness, and you will form a European brotherhood, just as Normandy, Brittany, Burgundy, Alsace and Lorraine—all our provinces—merged into France.'

When Victor Hugo published that utopia in 1850, his contemporaries considered him to be a fool and a dreamer. A Europe without nations?! The laughter was immense and derisive. Twenty years later, the Franco-Prussian War broke out. Things weren't so funny any more. These days, though, that idea describes our reality, the historic process in which we've been engaged for more than 60 years now.

Who said the following:

At no time was the separation of states in Europe greater. . . . Through ordinances, economic measures and autarky, states cordon themselves off in oppressive isolation. But as they do so, they're all aware of the fact that European economies and European politics share a common fate, and that no individual country can escape from a common world crisis through such separation. . . . Head to head in a decisive wrestling match, the two ideas—nationalism and supranationalism—stand in opposition. There's no retreating from the problem any more, and the immediate future will clearly show whether the European states persist in their present economic and political enmity or whether they want to solve their conflicts permanently through total unification in a supranational organization. . . . Will Europe continue its self-destruction or will it unify?

Stefan Zweig wrote that in 1932. As we all know, both things happened: continued self-destruction culminating in the complete devastation of the continent and the greatest crimes against humanity—and then, finally, the process of unification.

I could, beginning with Novalis (1772–1801) and moving forward, cite dozens of such quotes illustrating that poets have always thought more expansively than political pragmatists, proving that what, at the time, was considered to be crazy or, to put it more politely, utopian responded to a more sustainable rationality whereas the pragmatists perished pragmatically every time, along with their respective worlds beyond which they were never able to think.

Since it has become actual history, the European unification process has progressed considerably. And yet, once again we're seeing dark, low-hanging clouds, as if the sky—or, at the very least, the beautiful canopy of the European idea—were about to come crashing down upon us. A strong headwind emerged. And suddenly everything—or at least a lot of the things—we regarded as rational consequences drawn from historical catastrophes appeared questionable again. I don't need to enumerate the symptoms of the crisis here. The crisis is familiar. But it remains misunderstood. Accordingly, I don't want to recount anything that once again conjures up what the actual question is. Rather, I would like to accept the following challenge: to confront in these questionable times the questions of the EU sceptics—those who consider people like me to be odd birds—and provide answers to them.

Following countless interviews and discussions, I have compiled a list of Frequently Asked Questions. I will now attempt to consider and explore those questions in such a way that, taken together, they provide a reconstruction of an old yet conclusive answer to a major question: Why Europe?

The euro crisis led to an existential crisis of the entire EU. Why, after its long success story and its many accomplishments that are now considered givens, are people currently having greater doubts than ever about European integration?

They think the successes—to the extent they feel them economically and socially—are the results of their own efforts, diligence and prudence. And they view the crisis as the product of other people's failures—the failures of 'Brussels' or 'the Greeks' or whomever else. That's profoundly human. If I'm doing pretty well, then I don't think it's due to my having good circumstances. I think it's because I was diligent and did things properly. If suddenly I'm not doing as well, then, however, it's due to poor conditions. Something's wrong with the larger context. Somewhere, others have to be at fault. Peace and prosperity promote a sense of self; crises foster collective rage and an Us-versus-Them mentality. That's the hour of nationalism, the most perfidious form of Us versus Them. That also explains the renationalization evident among the opposition in the current EU crisis, since the EU is a decidedly postnational project. Of course, the fact that the growing desire for national sovereignty is logically and humanly understandable doesn't mean it's rational.

Isn't the retreat to the nation-state, to something smaller and more manageable, also a natural response when the larger entity is no longer clear and comprehensible?

The world, the big picture, was never clear and comprehensible, not even in the New Stone Age. That's why everyone cobbles together a worldview in which they know their way around and can find their way home. Nationalism is such a primitive navigator. You stumble through life. A martial voice says: 'Please turn around and then turn right.' And you think, now I finally know my way around. As a matter of fact, the 'nation' is just as complex and difficult to understand as any other model of human, social and political organization. The only difference is that we have the historical experience—which we must heed—that the nation produces criminal energy because it cannot create community without internal and external enemies and competitors. The European project was the consequence drawn from that experience. The desire to return to sovereign nation-states is thus not a natural response but a mindless and ahistorical one. But the mind and its consciousness are components of human nature. At least in theory . . .

Does affirming the nation automatically lead to nationalism? Must we indeed view the nation and everything connected to it only with an eye to the aberrations and cataclysmic wars of the nineteenth and twentieth centuries?

We can, of course, also see things differently. Enough people do that, you know. Nothing speaks against it—except, of course, our historical experiences. Can you have roast pork without a pig? It doesn't matter how appropriately you care for the pig; in the end, you still have roast pork. The more appropriate the care, the better the pork. A nation can never be so fortunate and peaceful that nationalism never raises its head. Especially in times of economic crises, nations develop aggressive dynamics. They terminate alliances, revise international treaties or invalidate them. Nowadays we see that particularly clearly in the UK's politics. We also see it in the mindless resentments Germany at present has towards 'the Greeks', and vice versa. Eventually, when so-called national interests can no longer be defended politically, the attempt is made to assert them with violence. Historical experience has taught us that it never leads to permanent success but it always does cause great suffering, including the destruction of lives, infrastructures and the means of production. In light of the contemporary, increasingly interconnected global situation, the notion that a nation can assert the interests of the majority of its population against those of others and succeed by being such an aggressive and solipsistic monad is completely absurd. Given the conditions according to which we organize ourselves and must lead our lives, everything happens transnationally: the flow of capital, the creation of values, ecology, communication and culture. As a result, what is the nation-state supposed to do? Wave those movements through? Even during the good times, when nationalism blithely appears as patriotism or love of one's homeland, nationalism—seen historically—is no longer innocent and never will be again. It's the political abuse of loving one's homeland.

What was the European ideal the founding fathers of the EU, Jean Monnet and Robert Schuman, had in mind? What was their vision? Above all, it had to do with peace.

That is correct, but that formulation only addresses half the truth. Monnet wrote that peace treaties between nations are not worth the paper they are printed on. He, along with the founding generation of the European project, had experienced four wars in his lifetime, all four of which were wars of national unification and wars of conquest. Peace treaties had preceded all those wars. Monnet's aspiration was thus to create true and lasting peace by surmounting the cause of those conflicts and wars: nationalism and, ultimately, the nation as a political reality and idea—the nation, that is, that defends its interests or, to be more precise, the interests of its elites, against all others. So how can you achieve that aspiration? His idea was to have the nations gradually cede increasing amounts of sovereignty rights to supranational institutions, until those nations eventually withered away. That is a bold, fascinating and radically enlightened idea, which we must always keep in mind when we talk about the EU. We shouldn't always just say 'peace project', because then no one thinks any more about the aspiration of overcoming nation-states.

Did that idea go far enough? Isn't it too utopian? Can it be we've reached a point that proves it just doesn't work?

Let's remember this: it hasn't gone far enough yet. That's right. That's the way historical processes work. A process is not a series of moments, each of which is successful and perfect in and of itself. Postnational development in Europe has progressed so far and the member states' economies have become so intertwined and interdependent that they can no longer solve a problem independently. Whichever nation-state attempts to assert its interests alone against the others only harms itself. That's good. That's the idea. That's how solidarity evolves. At the same time, the development still has not progressed far enough—that is, we're not yet at the point where larger problems that have emerged can actually be solved collectively. This no-longer-not-yet we're in right now is precisely what we call the crisis. While a common currency—which was a great step towards integration—was created, the national interests of individual EU member states obstructed the creation of the political instruments necessary to accompany that currency, namely, common economic, fiscal and monetary policies. The individual nation-states were not willing to cede so much sovereignty at the time. Now, they are painfully learning that, by defending their sovereignty in that way, they have commandingly caused great harm. Suddenly, there are resolutions that go far beyond what, during the initial decade of this century, was considered to be the pragmatic maximum possible. And that is just the beginning. To put it another way: the crisis is not a threat to Europe; the crisis will further the European project.

Why do those who call for 'more Europe' in order to deal with the crisis never concretely say what they mean by 'more Europe'?

'More Europe' is, in fact, as much an empty phrase as a necessity. As an empty phrase, the call is the opposite of a necessity as well as the opposite of the European idea—in other words, more competence for the European Council. In the European Council, the heads of state defend so-called national interests. The interests of the strongest ones literally become telling for the smaller ones. That doesn't promote postnational development: it undermines it. The political elites in Europe have difficulty saying what 'more Europe' concretely means for two reasons: either because they have forgotten what the idea of the European project is or because it touches upon the taboo of national democracy. Since they are only elected nationally, they cannot call national democracy into question. 'More

Europe' as a necessity and as a parameter for gauging euro-political decisions, however, must aggressively pose the question: What should a democratic Europe and its postnational democracy look like? That's the discussion of the future. And by having that discussion, it will be necessary to call everything into question. Everyone nods when they hear 'competitiveness in a globalized world'. I think that instead of nodding they should start shaking their heads—and thinking. For example: The single European market is so big—does an export economy really have to be the measure of all things? Or: Socially produced wealth is so great—shouldn't we pause and think about distributive justice instead of even more growth? And: Is growth really growth if it is paid for with debt?

Does surmounting the nation-states inevitably lead to the United States of Europe? And isn't it ultimately necessary to call an entity on the global scale of the USA, China or Brazil into question? Wouldn't yet another supernation-state come into being?

A supernation-state was never the idea. A United States of Europe modelled on the USA is a completely retro prospect. The USA is the old European project. What did the European immigrants do in the New World? It was classically old European: violently conquer territory, unify it through civil war and then form a nation. The EU is the new project, the contrary in every respect: voluntary accession, alignment through treaties and economic linkage, and dissolution of the nation-states. The USA was the avant-garde of the nineteenth century, the EU the avant-garde of the twenty-first.

Through globalization, haven't we created worldwide structures that, due to their complexity, we can no longer control and which increasingly plunge us into crises? Didn't it start with the worldwide financial crises and won't it end with the political inability to combat climate change?

The way things stand at the moment, globalization is, first and foremost, a rumour, an excuse for local political failure and the bogeyman of ahistorical thinking. If the average growth of international trade continues as it did for the past 15 years, then, in the year 2030, we'll once again reach the state of globalization of 1913. Economic historians know that. There are books about it. The problem is that people's memories don't include their grandparents' and great-grandparents' recollections and experiences. The problem is not so-called globalization. The problem, rather, is that globalization has been set back 150 years due to nationalistic wars and fascism.

Don't we conversely have to begin thinking more intensively in smaller, more comprehensible units?

We're doing that constantly. We always define ourselves according to the small structures in which we live. The region in which we grew up and were socialized defines our identity, not the fiction of the nation. You just have to learn to keep the following things in mind: the parameters you reasonably want to have in your region and the opportunities as well as the legal situation in the place you live. Those are in the interests of every person living on this continent. It cannot be the case that, in terms of how I shape my life, I have completely different interests than the people in Alentejo, Portugal or in the Peloponnese. I think it's possible to agree about that, without national resentments. Especially given the guarantees of freedom of movement and freedom of establishment on the continent, everyone has to have an interest in having the same parameters in effect everywhere, within which everyone's interests, that is, the interests of each individual, can freely develop. I said parameters. They do not preclude regional differences that have evolved or will evolve within those parameters based on distinct traditions, mentalities or other conditions. The diversity within common parameters belongs to Europe's richness; differences without common parameters, however, turn Europe into a strife-ridden and, in times of crises, aggressive continent, as we well know.

Moreover, in the long term, the EU is the system than can guarantee a life with comprehensible units and effective possibilities for participation. For all of the sovereignty the nation-state surrenders, the region receives many more rights in return, based on the principle of subsidiarity.

How can a European identity emerge, given the great cultural and linguistic differences in Europe? Isn't European integration doomed to fail because Europe has no common language? The hope that the euro could play a role in creating a sense of identity seems to have gone nowhere.

A common language is the standard of a nation-state. That's not what Europe is about. It's not a question of building a European nation. Linguistic and cultural diversity is one of

Europe's strengths. That kind of diversity creates identity where people live. European identity is nothing other than the security that the entire continent has enduringly agreed to: equal parameters, human rights, the rule of law, peace, social security and social justice. Those are the stakes defining the European project. Move among them and shape your life as a free person. The euro was a great step for postnational development: the first transnational currency in history! For the first time, states were willing to relinquish their national currencies for a joint project. The fact that the euro doesn't function well is due to an array of national egotisms and special interests that prevented the transnational currency from being politically managed supranationally. The crisis that resulted doesn't prove that the idea doesn't work. Rather, the crisis is further proof that nation-states produce crises.

After the fall of the Iron Curtain and its attending euphoria, did the eastern enlargement of the EU and the introduction of the euro occur too rapidly and without sufficient preparation? What lessons can be learnt from that?

The so-called eastern enlargement didn't proceed too quickly but, rather, too slowly. For example, Yugoslavia should have been incorporated immediately, without waiting until the country shattered into nation-states so that the new nations could then be admitted one by one to the postnational project. That would have avoided a civil war and the EU would have been enlarged with a community having experience with supranationality.

Shouldn't Europe grow much slower and with its citizens instead of without them and as an elitist project?

'Its citizens' is such an abstract term it's not even manageable any more. Who exactly are they supposed to be? Whenever the nationalists want to hide something, they now talk about the 'citizens', just like they used to talk about the 'Volk'. It's a scam, by virtue of which a bank director's spouse, as being part of the broad public, shares common interests with a factory worker from the same country. The outcome, as we know, was that workers ended up shooting at the workers from other countries and they bit the dust together. The question isn't slow or fast, or, with or without its citizens. Usually, you don't decide to implement a project slowly if you can do it quicker. You do it as quickly or slowly as the conditions, relative strength and possibilities allow. That determines the speed. I'm of the opinion that the lack of imagination among the current political elites is a much greater problem than the fact that there are, just as there always have been, political elites making the political decisions. Bold political elites set the European project in motion— and bequeathed it to a generation that neither knows its history nor has a vision of the future it should lead to. Those who now call themselves European politicians are not making any progress. And the worst part is they're riding roughshod over what has already been achieved.

Whether further communitarization proceeds slower or quicker, won't it, in any event, destroy the European democracy that has grown historically? That democracy was established by sovereign nation-states. But the more sovereignty rights those nation-states transfer to 'Brussels', the greater the losses their national parliaments suffer. Those parliaments are incrementally being disempowered, so to speak, while the European Commission, which has the right of initiative to propose laws in the EU, is only dubiously democratically legitimate.

First, there is no historically grown democracy in Europe. You can't make that kind of generalization. For the majority of European states, democracy was never something fought for and thus couldn't 'grow historically'. What we at present understand as democracy was implanted in the occupied countries by the victorious powers subsequent to the conclusion of wars or, following the implosion of authoritarian systems, plastered over the old structures by the old political elites as mimicry and so on. European democracies are covered with the birthmarks of authoritarian and feudal systems.

Second, even if the majority of national democracies in Europe had been or had become more ideal than they ultimately were, in the history of democracy, nation-state democracies constitute only one of the many democratic models we know of—and one that corresponded to a particular historical epoch that is now coming to a close. That model was theoretically the best possible structure for organizing human political participation in a nation-state. By transcending the nation-states, though, that particular model will perish as well. It's a completely normal historical process. Throughout history, forms of democratic organization have frequently ceased to exist once their preconditions ceased to exist. For example, the classical democracy of antiquity came to an end when its slave-holding society was superseded by a new social formation. No one wants that classical democracy back, even though we learnt in high school how wonderful it was, because no one wants to reinstitute a slaveholding society. We could go through all the eras in which democratic forms of organization were developed; they all had their own models, which ultimately always disappeared. The problem is not that the democracy—which, to some extent, we have practised and is familiar to us—is currently eroded. The problem, rather, is that we have not yet developed a sense of how to construct the model that will eventually supersede the national democracies. In Europe, something historically completely new is coming into existence: the first postnational continent. It can only work, though, if we also develop a new model of democracy that corresponds to that historical development. The greatest democratic deficits in the current construction of the EU could be rectified swiftly and easily. It's true that the European Commission has a legitimation problem. That could be resolved if the commissioners were elected by the European Parliament. That, in turn, would necessitate that the European Parliament be endowed with all the powers a developed parliamentarianism requires—including the linchpin of parliamentarianism: sovereign budgetary power. In order for that to happen, it must also become possible for the EU to generate its own budget, instead of being dependent upon the contributions of member states, whose heads of government regularly fight over reducing their contributions so as to be able to present themselves to their constituents in the nation-state as defenders of national interests while, again in the name of national interests, they clamour for increased support which Brussels should return to the nation-states. That unproductive contradiction fuels aggressions, and that contradiction can only be resolved by a new model of democracy which takes as its starting point the idea of the community— instead of the nation. Thus we clearly see that, if we begin our discussion of democracy by considering the democratic legitimacy of the Commission, we arrive at the Parliament—and the issue of what powers the European Parliament requires and so on. It takes us from one thing to another, and with each step we see the contradictions in our accustomed national democracy—while our experiences with that accustomed national democracy also enable us to gradually imagine a postnational democracy.

Isn't there a danger that, in transferring national parliamentary powers to Brussels, a centralized superstate will emerge? One that definitely no one wants because it would be too far removed from its citizens, ignorant about all local needs and inflexible about regional specifics, and would thus just lump everything together?

In point of fact, no one wants that. It's not inherent to the aspirations and dynamics of the development. The fact is that the national parliaments have already ceded about 80 per cent of their sovereignty rights to supranational organizations. Among the remaining 20 per cent are some very big chunks, for example, budgetary powers, fiscal policy and so on. But it's also a fact that, due to the current crisis, these remaining, weighty national rights are also being perforated, weakened and, ultimately, yielded. The

continuing loss of influence among national parliaments, however, leads to the increased importance and possibilities of
regional parliaments. National parliaments will pass, and
regional parliaments will become more significant. To allege
that the EU will lead to centralism and the nation-state, in contrast, guarantees subsidiarity is absurd. The majority of EU
member states, especially large ones like France and Poland,
are organized extremely centralistically whereas the Commission in all those states systematically operates regionally. The
principle of subsidiarity is codified in the Treaty of Lisbon. It
has not yet been defined or brought before the Court of Justice
of the European Union. That also means, though, that Leopold
Kohr's vision of having small and interconnected democratic
administrative units (whether we call them 'states', 'regions' or
something else), for example, has never in history had a greater
chance of being instituted than it does now. It's the task and
the opportunity of regional parliaments to insist on that possibility and expand their sphere of influence step by step. The
internal dynamics of the EU provide the members of regional
parliaments with increasingly greater importance than the
members of national parliaments. Once the members of
regional parliaments realize that, reality will succumb. At that
point, the bold dream can come true: Europe as the first postnational continent in world history, peacefully organized in a
free association of self-determining regions based on human
rights and with common parameters developed and protected
by supranational institutions in Brussels.

For those who object that this is too idealistic, it's necessary
to provide the following response: ideals have consistently

served throughout history as the impetus for the greatest advances in freedom. Whoever dismisses idealism as totally unrealistic, however, has to explain why pragmatism is currently destroying so many real values.

One last question: Whatever happened to the sparrow I talked about at the beginning? Well, at some point, the tomcat strayed back to the meadow where he had had the encounter with the little bird lying on his back, his little legs in the air. The cat wanted to know if he was still lying there, what he was doing now and whether he had another eccentric idea. The cat, however, couldn't find him. The clouds had blown over. A radiant sky arched high above the lush meadow. Perhaps it hadn't even been a bird, but the angel of history, whom the storm, which had been blowing, had carried away long ago. The meadow was teeming with life. Everything was glittering merrily in the sun. And over there—the cat couldn't believe his eyes—wasn't that a lamb lying peacefully beside a wolf?

But I'll just dream on—and leave it at that!

ADAC. Allgemeiner Deutscher Automobil-Club, a German automobile club, also Europe's largest.

Bay of Pigs. Failed US military attack on Cuba in 1961. The goal of the invasion was to overthrow the revolutionary government of Fidel Castro.

Berlaymont building. Headquarters of the European Commission in Brussels.

Brüning, Heinrich (1885–1970). German imperial chancellor (1930–32) from the conservative Centre Party, who frequently suspended Reichstag legislation through emergency decrees.

Court of Justice of the European Union. Responsible for interpreting EU laws and ensuring they are administered equally in all EU countries. Its headquarters is located in Luxembourg.

DSDS. Deutschland sucht den Superstar or *Germany Searches for Its Superstar*, a German television programme, similar to *American Idol*, in which a panel of judges and audience voting select Germany's best singer.

EEC. European Economic Community, founded by the signing of the Treaty of Rome in 1957. In 1993 (with the Maastricht Treaty), it was renamed the European Community (EC). Once the Treaty of Lisbon became law in 2009, it ceased to exist as a separate entity.

European Commission. The executive body of the EU, the European Commission represents the interests of the EU as a whole (as opposed to the interests of the individual countries). Every 5 years, its 28 commissioners (one from each member state) are newly appointed. The European Council nominates a candidate to be president of the Commission, who must be approved by a majority of the members of the European Parliament. The president assigns the remaining commissioners to their area of responsibility. Those nominations, in turn, must be approved by the Council of Ministers and the Parliament. The main office of the European Commission is located in Brussels.

European Council. Sets the general political objectives and priorities of the EU. It influences the determination of the EU's political agenda, but is not, however, competent to enact legislation. Its members consist of the heads of state of the countries belonging to the EU, the current president of the European Commission and the president of the European Council. The High Representative of the Union for Foreign Affairs and Security Policy participates in the Council's meetings as well.

European Parliament. Together with the Council of the European Union, the Parliament constitutes the legislative authority of the EU. The members of Parliament represent Europe's citizens and are directly elected every five years.

FRG. The Federal Republic of Germany, formally established in 1949 in what had been the American, British and French zones of occupation following the Second World War. The country was frequently referred to as West Germany until German unification in 1990.

GDR. The German Democratic Republic, formally established in 1949 in what had been the Soviet Occupation Zone following the Second World War. The country was frequently referred to as East Germany until it became part of the Federal Republic of Germany in 1990.

GNTM. Germany's next Topmodel, a television show in which former international model Heidi Klum searches for a successor.

Invasion of Grenada. In October 1983, the US military invaded the Caribbean nation of Grenada. The intervention is also known as Operation Urgent Fury.

GZSZ. Gute Zeiten, schlechte Zeiten or *Good Times, Bad Times,* a successful German television series that began in 1992.

IMF. International Monetary Fund, a specialized agency of the United Nations, created in 1945. Its purpose is to facilitate cooperation on issues regarding the international monetary system and to provide mutual financial assistance to overcome balance-of-payment difficulties.

Josephinism. A form of enlightened absolutism under Habsburg emperor Joseph II (1741–90), which led to legal, administrative, educational, cultural and, especially, religious reforms. Frequently referred to as a 'revolution from above'.

Kfz. Kraftfahrzeug, a German synonym for automobile.

London Conference. The Conference on German External Debts (1952) led to the London Debt Agreement, signed in 1953, addressing German payment obligations following the Second World War (prewar and postwar debts). Issues of reparations were postponed for a subsequent peace treaty which never came into existence. The Two-Plus-Four Treaty was signed in 1990 instead.

Maastricht Treaty. Signed in 1992 in Maastricht, Netherlands, by 12 members of the European Community, the treaty, officially known as the Treaty on European Union (TEU), came into force in 1993.

Montanunion. Another term for the European Coal and Steel Community (ECSC). Since 1992 (the Maastricht Treaty), it is an integrative component of the European Union.

OEEC. The Organisation for European Economic Co-operation, established in 1948 to carry out the Marshall Plan. Superseded in 1960 by the OECD, the Organisation for Economic Co-operation and Development.

Subsidiarity. From Latin *subsidium* (support, assistance). A sociopolitical concept according to which a higher-level authority (for example, a community of states) should only assume those tasks that cannot be performed at a more local (for example, an individual state) level.

Treaties of Rome. In force since 1958, they consist of the Treaty establishing the European Economic Community (TEEC) and the Treaty establishing the European Atomic Energy Community (EURATOM) as well as the agreement concerning the communal entities of the European Community. Signed in Rome by Belgium, France, Italy, Luxembourg, the Netherlands and West Germany.

Treaty of Lisbon. International treaty between the 28 member states of the EU signed in Lisbon in 2007 during the Portuguese Council presidency. It came into force in 2009.

TÜV. Technischer Überwachungsverein, the organization that, among other things, administers German drivers' licence tests and also oversees automobile inspections in Germany.